STUCK IN TRANSIT
Rethinking Russian Economic Reform

Centre for Economic Policy Research (CEPR)

90–98 Goswell Road
London, EC1V 7RR
UK

Tel: (44 20) 878 2900
Fax: (44 20) 878 2999
Email: cepr@cepr.org
Website: http://www.cepr.org

HC
340.12
.S784
1999

Russian European Centre for Economic Policy (RECEP)

Potapovsky Pereulok 5, Building 4
101000 Moscow
Russian Federation

Tel: (7 095) 232 3613
Fax: (7 095) 232 3739
Email: recep@recep.glasnet.ru

Stockholm Institute of Transition Economics and East European Economies (SITE)

Stockholm School of Economics
Sveavägen 65, Box 6501
S-113 83 Stockholm
Sweden

Tel: (46 8) 736 9670
Fax: (46 8) 31 6422
Email: Minea.Hedlund@hhs.se
Website: http://www.hhs.se/site

British Library Cataloguing in Publication Data

A catalogue record for this book is available from the British Library

ISBN 1 898128 44 8

Prepared and printed by Keyword Publishing Services Ltd

© European Commission

STUCK IN TRANSIT
Rethinking Russian Economic Reform

The Russian European Centre for Economic Policy (RECEP) is a bright new member of the international research community and a front-line revitalizing force in the renewal of Russian economic research. This Report presents some of its recent work on the policy options for rebuilding the Russian economy, particularly in the light of the financial crisis of August 1998 and the deep flaws it exposed in the process of reform.

Edited by

Erik Berglöf
Stockholm Institute of Transition Economics and East European Economies (SITE)
Russian European Centre for Economic Policy (RECEP)
Centre for Economic Policy Research (CEPR)

Romesh Vaitilingam
Independent writer and consultant

The RECEP project is financed by the European Union's Tacis programme, which provides grant finance for know-how to foster the development of market economies and democracy in the New Independent States and Mongolia.

Centre for Economic Policy Research

The Centre for Economic Policy Research is a network of almost 500 Research Fellows, based primarily in European universities. The Centre coordinates its Fellows' research activities and communicates their results to the public and private sectors. CEPR is an entrepreneur, developing research initiatives with the producers, consumers and sponsors of research. Established in 1983, CEPR is a European economics research organization with uniquely wide-ranging scope and activities.

CEPR is a registered educational charity. Institutional (core) finance for the Centre is provided by major grants from the Economic and Social Research Council, under which an ESRC Resource Centre operates within CEPR; the Esmée Fairbairn Charitable Trust and the Bank of England. The Centre is also supported by the European Central Bank; the Bank for International Settlements; 22 national central banks and 45 companies. None of these organizations gives prior review to the Centre's publications, nor do they necessarily endorse the views expressed therein.

The Centre is pluralist and non-partisan, bringing economic research to bear on the analysis of medium- and long-run policy questions. CEPR research may include views on policy, but the Executive Committee of the Centre does not give prior review to its publications, and the Centre takes no institutional policy positions. The opinions expressed in this report are those of the authors and not those of the Centre for Economic Policy Research.

Executive Committee
Co-Chairmen Guillermo de la Dehesa
                Anthony Loehnis

Jan Krysztof Bielecki	Denis Gromb	Mario Sarcinelli
Diane Coyle	Philippe Lagayette	Kermit Schoenholtz
Quentin Davies MP	Peter Middleton	Philippe Weil
Bernard Dewe Mathews	Rafael Repullo	
Francesco Giavazzi	Bridget Rosewell	

Officers
President   Richard Portes
Chief Executive Officer Stephen Yeo

Research Director   Mathias Dewatripont

November 1999

Stockholm Institute of Transition Economics and East European Economies

SITE is an international centre for advanced research in economics located at the Stockholm School of Economics. The Institute's mission is to be a source of knowledge for – and about – the economies in transition. The research focus is on the institutional challenges facing transition economies. SITE aims to put research results to use, sharing the accumulated experience of transition with governments and businesses involved in the development of these countries.

An increasingly important part of SITE's mission is to assist the countries in transition in developing their own centres of research and knowledge. Under SITE's leadership, the Russian European Centre for Economic Policy (RECEP) has become one of the few research institutes making use of the tools of modern economics in Russia. At RECEP, a new generation of young Russian economists is shaping economic policy and contributing to public debate in the country. Through the RECEP project, SITE places its international academic network at the disposal of these future leaders of Russian government, business and academe. SITE is pursuing similar initiatives in other transition countries, for example in the Baltic region.

SITE is a private, non-profit foundation. Core funding is provided in the form of long-term grants from the Swedish government and from nine companies and banks: ABB, AGA, Axel Johnson, Ericsson, Merita Nordbanken, Skandinaviska Enskilda Banken, Svenska Handelsbanken, Tetra Laval and Volvo. Additional funding is provided by private businesses and banks in the form of annual subscription fees, and by the European Commission and research foundations in the form of project grants.

SITE Board of Trustees
Göran Ennerfelt (*Chairman*), President and CEO, Axel Johnson AB
Michael Sohlman (*Vice Chairman*), Executive Director, The Nobel Foundation
Hans Dalborg, President and CEO, Merita Nordbanken
Ann Uustalu, Deputy Assistant Under-Secretary of State, Swedish Ministry for Foreign Affairs
Claes-Robert Julander, President, Stockholm School of Economics
Sven-Eric Söder, Under-Secretary of State, Swedish Ministry for Foreign Affairs

Erik Berglöf, SITE Director and RECEP Project Director

Contents

List of Contributors	xi
Preface	xiii
1 Russia's Crisis and Beyond	**1**
Decline and fall	2
The failure of debt conversion	3
Recovery	4
Exchange rate economics	5
The economics of politics	7
2 Macroeconomic Policy and the Problem of Arrears	**9**
Tight fiscal and monetary policy	9
Arrears	10
Policy implications	12
3 Tax Collection and Fiscal Federalism	**15**
Can't tax or won't tax?	15
The fiscal crisis	15
Russia's tax capacity	17
Inter-governmental relations	19
Federal–regional relations	20
Sub-regional relations	20
Policy implications	21
4 Banking and the Financial–Industrial Groups	**23**
The banking crisis	23
The emergence of FIGs	23
Roles of FIGs	24
Increasing the productivity of capital where legal institutions are weak	24
Substituting for missing or highly imperfect capital markets	25
Improving production performance through economies of scale	25
Minimizing price distortions resulting from state interference in markets	25
The drawbacks of a FIG-dominated economy	25
FIG membership and economic performance	26
Restructuring Russia's banks	27

5 Industrial Restructuring	**31**
Does market structure matter?	31
What can the state do for industrial firms?	33
Policies to encourage restructuring	33
Increased competition in the product market	34
The hardening of bank–firm credit	34
Enforcement of bankruptcy laws	35
6 Labour Market Reform	**37**
Wage arrears	37
Labour regulation	39
Enforcement	40
Reforming the regulatory framework of industrial relations	41
7 Russia's Barter Economy	**43**
Every enterprise uses barter	44
Explaining the use of barter	44
Is barter good or bad?	46
Policy implications	46
Bibliography	**49**

List of Contributors

Rudiger Ahrend, *RECEP*
Erik Berglöf, *SITE, RECEP and CEPR*
Annette Brown, *Western Michigan University and RECEP*
John S. Earle, *SITE and Central European University*
Guido Friebel, *SITE, RECEP and CEPR*
Maria Gorban, *RECEP*
Irena Grosfeld, *RECEP, DELTA and CEPR*
Sergei Guriev, *RECEP*
Barry W. Ickes, *New Economic School*
Nadezhda Ivanova, *RECEP*
Simon Johnson, *MIT and RECEP*
Rory MacFarquhar, *RECEP*
Dalia Marin, *University of Munich and CEPR*
Damien Neven, *RECEP, University of Lausanne and CEPR*
Enrico Perotti, *RECEP, University of Amsterdam and CEPR*
Claudia Senik-Leygonie, *RECEP and DELTA*
Peter Westin, *RECEP*
Charles Wyplosz, *RECEP, Graduate Institute of International Studies, Geneva, and CEPR*
Ksenia Yudaeva, *RECEP and SITE*
Katherina Zhuravskaya, *RECEP*

Preface

The Russian European Centre for Economic Policy (RECEP) is a bright new member of the international research community and a front-line revitalizing force in the renewal of Russian economic research. This Report presents some of its recent work on the policy options for rebuilding the Russian economy, particularly in the light of the financial crisis of August 1998 and the deep flaws it exposed in the process of reform.

RECEP's development has been remarkable. In less than two years since the Stockholm Institute of Transition Economics (SITE), leading a consortium with the Centre for Economic Policy Research (CEPR) and the Département et Laboratoire d'Economie Théoriques et Appliquées (DELTA) in Paris, undertook to build RECEP into a modern research centre and policy think-tank, it has become a unique entity in Russia.* It is one of the few centres in the country where modern analytical tools are applied to produce top-quality economic research and policy advice. And it is the only institution, private or public, that has managed to attract back Russian graduates from leading doctoral programmes in the West.

The Centre now has a critical mass of young well-trained Russian economists working with Western experts on the best set of databases available in Russia. These young Russians successfully compete for presentations at international conferences and publication in leading academic journals. But they also regularly participate in outreach activities in less privileged environments, such as Ekaterinburg, Voronezh, Nizhny Novgorod and St Petersburg.

In 1998, RECEP was the most successful individual institution in Russia-wide competitions for research project grants awarded by the Economics Education Research Consortium. RECEP papers were selected for presentation in tough international competition at both the 1998 and 1999 annual meetings of the European Economic Association and the 1999 annual Conference on Transition in Beijing hosted by the William Davidson Institute at the University of Michigan, CEPR and the World Bank. And in late 1999, a paper on fiscal federalism by Katherina Zhuravskaya won the Young Economist Competition sponsored by the Nobel Foundation and was the only paper selected for presentation at the fifth Nobel Symposium in Economics, *The Economics of Transition*, in September 1999.

Despite a turbulent political scene, RECEP maintains strong links to Russian policy-makers in key government institutions. Working relationships take the form of policy memoranda, requested from government bodies or at RECEP's own

---

* RECEP grew into a centralized research centre thanks to a large project grant from the Tacis programme of the European Commission. In a seminal retention effort, a multi-year grant from the Fanny and Leo Koerner Foundation provides core support for RECEP's academic faculty. RECEP also benefits from research project grants and academic exchange programmes.

initiative, meetings on a broad range of policy issues, and cooperation in construction of large in-house databases. RECEP economists also work closely with the international financial institutions, most recently in projects focusing on the restructuring of the Russian banking sector.

Through the journal *Russian Economic Trends*, the leading international source of information on the Russian economy, RECEP disseminates research and information to a broad audience inside Russia and internationally

see   www.hhs.se/site/ret/ret.htm

or

www.blackwellpublishers.co.uk/ruet.

At monthly press conferences, RECEP researchers and Russian policy-makers shed light on key policy issues, and the Centre also organizes regular 'RECEPtions', where policy-makers and academics exchange ideas. Through visibility in Russian and international media, RECEP aims to contribute to the raising of public awareness about the economic situation in Russia and the measures required to rebuild its economy.

In September 1998, RECEP hosted its first annual international conference, *Economic and Social Reform: A European–Russian Dialogue*. The conference was held in Moscow in the immediate aftermath of the financial crisis and during a serious political shake-up. Nearly 20 academic papers addressed the many problems facing transition economies, with special attention to Russia's plight. This Report summarizes the discussion and findings of the conference as well as incorporating newer material from RECEP's output to shed light on the traumatic events and their underlying causes.

Erik Berglöf
Director, SITE and RECEP
November 1999

1 Russia's Crisis and Beyond

Nineteen ninety-eight was supposed to be the year of a push for reform in Russia after years of inactivity and before campaign fever once again paralysed the political process. The symbol of 'nomenklatura capitalism', Viktor Chernomyrdin, had been fired from the job of prime minister by President Yeltsin and young Sergei Kiriyenko had been appointed to lead the government. The 'reformers' were back.

But on 17 August 1998, Russia's economy was finally punished for its delays in reform, its lack of fiscal discipline and its overvalued exchange rate when the government was forced to devalue the rouble and default on its debt obligations. In the immediate aftermath of the crisis, many forecasters predicted hyper-inflation and a large and rapid fall in production. Viktor Gerashchenko, dubbed 'the world's worst central banker' by Jeffrey Sachs, had been re-appointed as governor of the Central Bank of Russia (CBR) and he was expected to resort once again to printing money.

Fortunately, this gloomy scenario has not yet materialized. Instead, the Russian economy has been on a path of recovery with impressive growth rates in industrial production, albeit from a low base and mainly in import-substituting activities. Inflation has come down, and Gerashchenko's actions have been very different from those taken in 1992–4, with monetary emissions kept at a reasonable level. There is, however, another side to Gerashchenko's record that is equally telling: there has been complete inaction on restructuring the failed banking sector. Put simply, Russia is now experiencing economic growth without structural reform.

More profoundly, the crisis has shifted international attention away from the successes of Russian reform – stabilization of the macroeconomy, the growth of the financial sector and the establishment of a fledgling democracy – to the failures. Economic output as measured by official statistics has fallen by more than 50% since the beginning of transition. Even if these figures are highly uncertain, over the same time period, life expectancy has fallen by four to five years, in contrast with most economies in the West where it has increased by one to two years. Inequality has increased dramatically and one half of the population has fallen below the critical mark of $4 a day used by the World Bank. More than 60% of children are living in households below this mark. And the rule of law is far from established with enforcement being the key problem. Russia ranks fourth from the bottom on international comparisons of corruption.

The list of troubling statistics could be made much longer. Most of them were more or less unaffected by the August 1998 crisis, but the financial collapse shifted the focus of foreign observers and, more importantly, dealt a serious blow to the constituency for reform. It also became clear to the West that the political landscape was more complex than a simple divide between reformers and anti-reformers.

The intermingling of business interests and politics, of personal enrichment and public service, has gradually been unveiled and the illusion has gone. The year of opportunity turned into a year of financial collapse, but also of a fundamental challenge to the approach of Russian reforms.

This chapter briefly summarizes the story of the crisis with a focus on the macroeconomic variables. It also gives some views on where the Russian economy now stands over a year after the default and devaluation. Later chapters look more closely at the underlying causes of Russia's vulnerability to external shocks and its failure to implement reforms.

Decline and fall

What precipitated the crisis? By mid-1997, the fall in production seemed to have bottomed out. Macroeconomic indicators in Russia were approaching those of other more successful transition economies: interest rates had declined to record low levels of below 20% and inflation was quickly approaching the single-digit range. The government had managed to bring down the high inflation of the early 1990s through a feat of financial engineering: by changing the way it financed budget deficits. The shift from direct monetary financing by the CBR to private sector loans in the form of short-term Treasury bills (GKOs), Eurobonds and other interest-bearing financial instruments led to a steady disinflation and bought the government time to try and rectify its fiscal imbalances.

Yet, at the same time, this strategy exposed the government to the ruthless judgement of the domestic – and later, international – financial markets. As long as investors believed that the government would be able to service its debt, investors were willing to roll over these loans. But when investors began to doubt that the government would be able to bring down the deficit rapidly enough to prevent the debt from growing out of control, there was going to come a point when the government would face the cumulative effect of its deferred decisions. That point was reached in the summer of 1998.

What went wrong? In economic terms, the situation was very simple. GKOs and Eurobonds were the debt of the Russian government and so their value was based on the federal government's ability to raise revenue. In the face of dwindling tax receipts – federal tax collection had fallen from 20% of GDP in 1992 to 8% in 1998 – the public debt was increasingly viewed as default grade. This was not because of a temporary shortfall in tax revenues but the symptom of a generalized loss of payment discipline, which included the build-up of pervasive payment arrears. A corrupt and highly inefficient tax service was letting profit-reporting firms evade payments. At the same time, the highest authorities were unable or unwilling to prosecute tax evaders, in particular large corporations, instead offering tax amnesties at regular intervals.

The public debt was held by three groups of investors: the state-owned savings bank, Sberbank; private Russian banks and firms, and foreigners. The foreigners seemed to believe in indefinite IMF bail-outs. Private Russian bankers were rushing for the exit, off-loading GKOs and using the proceeds to buy dollars and invest abroad. Their counterparts were Sberbank, which was officially trying to defend the value of GKOs, but in fact was bailing out the bankers, and the CBR, which was providing the dollars out of reserves that were fast drying up. By the end of June, there were no buyers of GKOs or roubles. The IMF then pledged another $10 billion but as soon as the loan reached Moscow, capital flight resumed in an endgame frenzy. Less than a month later, the CBR had to abandon the rouble, which lost half its value in a week and went on depreciating to around a quarter of its July 1998 value.

Two changes in the world economy contributed to the timing of the crisis: contagion from the Asian financial crisis, which had begun in July of the previous year, and declining commodity prices, particularly the price of oil. Commodities make up about 80% of Russia's exports and the drops in price caused exports to fall by 10% in the first half of 1998 compared with the first half of 1997. The combination of large inflows of short-term foreign portfolio capital and weak protection of investor rights made Russia very vulnerable to external shocks.

But Russia's vulnerabilities went deeper and were largely of its own making (see RECEP, 1998). The necessary pressures for enterprise restructuring were still weak. The banking sector was fragile. There was a history of direct or indirect government subsidies to enterprises and bail-outs of inter-enterprise arrears. And privatization had been pushed through in an environment of endemic corruption and without adequate respect for the rule of law.

The failure of debt conversion

The Russian government did try to avert the crisis. In mid-July 1998, one month before the August default and devaluation, it made a last-ditch attempt to restore confidence in the rouble-denominated market for GKOs. With nominal yields on the instruments averaging 63% in 1996, 26% in 1997 and soaring again in the early part of 1998, the nominal value of the market had snowballed to around $70 billion by June 1998, of which $55 billion was the interest component alone. It was clear that something had to be done and the choice was between converting some of the GKOs into either long-term rouble paper or dollar-denominated paper.

The Russian government chose the second option and organized a swap of GKOs for Eurobonds. In total, R27.5 billion in GKOs were converted into $4.4 billion in Eurobonds. The swap promised to decrease debt service in the forthcoming year and, since GKO yields to maturity were much higher than Eurobond yields, to decrease the interest costs of the total debt (GKOs and Eurobonds). The hope was that the swap would also help restore confidence in Russian financial markets, staving off the threat of devaluation.

Research by Ksenia Yudaeva and Charles Wyplosz, presented at the RECEP conference, estimates the costs and benefits of the debt swap from rouble to dollar instruments. The direct interest costs were equal to 2.83% in dollar terms, net of the premium for lengthening debt maturity. But this cost was initially outweighed by the positive effect of the swap on Russian financial markets. Unfortunately, the improvements on the markets did not last and any gains were swamped under massive capital losses when the rouble devalued (see Yudaeva and Wyplosz, 1998; and Yudaeva, 1998).

The Russian experience of converting local currency-denominated debts into dollar-denominated debts reinforces the lessons from Mexico's similar efforts in 1994. Such financial engineering can delay but not avert devaluation, and the gain in time is ultimately very costly, since the damage done by devaluation becomes that much greater. It also appears that the conversion tends to decrease investor confidence in foreign currency-denominated debts and to increase the interest rate on such debts without producing a fall in the interest costs of domestic debts.

Recovery

Writing in *Russian Economic Trends* more than a year on from the crisis, Peter Westin notes that Russia's producers and exporters can look back at two particular events that have provided the foundation for the industrial recovery and healthy export environment since August 1998. One is the devaluation of the rouble; the other is the agreement made by OPEC in March 1999 to limit world oil supply, bringing surging world market oil prices (see Westin, 1999).

A devaluation of this magnitude does give domestic producers and exporters a competitive edge. For Russia, this has materialized in the form of strong growth in industrial production, driven mainly by import substitution and an improved situation for exporters, many of whom have their costs in roubles but their revenues in dollars. But a devaluation also has negative effects, undermining a country's ability to service its external debt and damaging the credibility of the currency. Domestic demand has also been damaged. Real wages were 36% lower in July 1999 compared to a year previously and the average monthly pension, which in July 1998 stood at R402.60 ($64.40), was R448.70 ($18.40) a year later. At the same time, the government's demand has been constrained by large debt payments.

The weaker rouble has been accompanied by only moderate inflation with the result that the real exchange rate has depreciated 43% since July 1998. The devaluation has had a positive impact on Russia's current account and trade balance, mainly due to the effect on imports, which in the first half of 1999 were down 45% compared to the first half of 1998. But exports have been unable to surpass 1998's level, and were down 12% in the first half of 1999, although they are increasingly helped by rising world commodity prices. Although the rouble has started to appreciate in real terms, a return to the pre-crisis level should not be expected in the near term. The effect of the devaluation and the continued depreciation does not yet seem to be over, though it is vital to emphasize that sustainable long-term growth must be accompanied by institutional reforms and enterprise restructuring.

Almost a year after the crisis, Russia received a new $4.5 billion credit line with the IMF, to be disbursed over a period of 18 months. This can be seen as a victory for both the IMF and the Russian government. In August 1998, Russia's ability to service its debt to the IMF was at risk and a default would have severely damaged the Fund's credibility: since 1993, it has lent Russia more than $20 billion, making the country its largest debtor. For Russia, which desperately needs foreign direct investment, the new loan gives it a sign of commitment and credibility, which in the case of a widespread default would have been completely lost. But the fact that the IMF essentially lent money for Russia to fulfil its payment obligations to the same organization points to the fundamental weakness of IMF conditionality, at least in Russia.

Russia's total external debt amounts to approximately $150 billion, close to 90% of its GDP. An agreement with the London and Paris Clubs on the Soviet debt, made possible by the IMF agreement, will be an important component in facilitating economic recovery. Without any debt restructuring, Russia's total debt obligations will range between $13–18 billion a year to the year 2008, making default highly probable. A deal has been announced with the Paris Club, which does not involve any write-offs; instead, there will be a two-year postponement of payments in which time Russia will only pay around $600 million.

Negotiations with the London Club creditors may turn out to be more problematic: first, 600 creditors have to agree to any deal; second, London Club debt has already been restructured once; and third, the creditors are still unhappy with Russia's restructuring deal for GKOs. Furthermore, revelations about large-scale corruption, rumoured to involve IMF funds, may delay the next IMF tranche and could have negative consequences for negotiations with creditors.

Exchange rate economics

Writing in *Russian Economic Trends*, Rudiger Ahrend explores the impact of the changing value of the rouble on Russia's decline, fall and recovery during 1996–9. He argues that coverage of Russia in Western newspapers gives the impression that the place is doomed, with commentators focusing on corruption and the absence of the rule of law as the main causes of the crisis. In fact, these two problems neither explain the crash nor the real news of recent months: that production in Russia is steadily growing for the first time in a decade. The reason for this turnaround is the collapse of the rouble, which freed industry from the uncompetitiveness of the former exchange rate (see Ahrend, 1999).

The depression of Russia's heartland in 1996–8 was largely caused by the very success of stabilization. To bring down rampant inflation, the exchange rate was pegged. This strategy is effective in reducing inflation, but it also means that the real exchange rate appreciates and consumption booms, fuelled by capital inflows and increased purchasing power. The drawback is that the competitiveness of the domestic economy deteriorates as the currency appreciates, and the current account goes into deficit. Later, it becomes very difficult to regain competitiveness through devaluation, since both politics and finance demand a continuation of the strong exchange rate.

Russia followed this pattern precisely: inflation was reduced and consumption and financial booms in 1997 triggered a small growth blip while industry continued to sink. Russia's one peculiarity was its continued current account surplus. The surplus did deteriorate, but the fact that there was a surplus made the rouble's value appear fair. With hindsight, it has become clear that large-scale capital flight made the current account surplus virtual and as unsustainable as what was happening in the real economy.

Many argue that the corrupt nature of Russia's political and economic system was the main reason why the old exchange rate turned out to be too high for domestic industry. But the problem of corruption has been evident for years, and it is hard to understand why observers only noticed after August 1998 that corruption had sabotaged the exchange rate policy. Clearly, if Russia had developed a more business-friendly environment, its industry could have afforded a somewhat higher real exchange rate without losing competitiveness. But keeping an overvalued exchange rate and waiting for corruption levels to go down is a clear suicide strategy. Improving corporate governance and the administrative and judicial systems are far bigger tasks than simply privatizing industry at knock-down prices, and will require years if not decades to complete.

But, while financial markets were booming, Ahrend claims the real economy was suffering from Russia's version of the 'Dutch Disease'. The Soviets had left an economy that was deeply divided: a rich mineral sector, primarily oil and gas, made up the bulk of its exports and provided the means to keep inefficient loss-making enterprises alive through explicit and implicit subsidies. This dual structure was reinforced and exacerbated by the overvalued exchange rate of the stabilization years. While the commodity-based export sector prospered, largely freed from providing subsidies, Russian manufacturing went from bad to worse. Companies made more losses and, in order to survive, they failed to pay taxes, wages and suppliers, and turned to barter. While corruption and tax avoidance were – and are – pervasive, they alone do not explain the growth of these 'virtual' phenomena.

Another consequence of the overvalued rouble was the inability of the federal government to reduce the budget deficit. Even though expenditures were cut drastically – which was reflected in the build-up of wage and pension arrears – the government was notoriously unable to collect sufficient taxes to balance the budget. This inability was mainly due to the depression of the real economy, for which the strong exchange rate was largely to blame.

Post-crisis, things are different. Federal tax revenues were up from 11% of GDP in the first half of 1998 to 13.1% of GDP in the first half of 1999, allowing the government to pay off some of its outstanding arrears: in June 1999, government wage arrears were 40% lower than their peak, and pension arrears had fallen by 70%. In the private sector, profits, cash-flow and order book levels are up, while barter and wage arrears are down. With a competitive exchange rate, the Russian economy is reviving for the first time in decades.

With hindsight, Russia's decline under an overvalued exchange rate and its revival since the crisis corrected the overvaluation are not very surprising. What is surprising is that, unlike many other countries that have followed this path in recent years (such as the UK, Mexico, Korea and Thailand), Russia has not gone through a major recession in the wake of the currency crisis and prior to recovery. On the contrary, the slump has been extremely short-lived, with the economy basically starting to recover in the second quarter after the crisis.

Ahrend concludes that the explanation for this surprising phenomena is that, unlike the others, Russia was not hit with a credit crunch after its crisis. Before the crisis, Russian banks mainly channelled money from local depositors and abroad into GKOs and the booming stock market. Lending money to the real sector was considered too risky, given the poor development of creditor rights, the dire state of industry and the enormous 'risk-free' gains that could be made in and around the GKO market. As a result, credit to the Russian real sector was unaffected by the crisis, since it had been largely non-existent beforehand.

The economics of politics

Russia's economic recovery does not seem to have been affected by political turmoil. Writing in *Russian Economic Trends*, Peter Westin notes that in the two years since early 1998, the country has seen four prime ministers lose their jobs but the markets have shrugged it off as 'business as usual'. Why is this? First, Russia's constitution gives the president almost exclusive decision-making power and the role of prime minister is less notable: although dismissal of the prime minister automatically means the end of the government, the changes in cabinet are much less dramatic. Second, markets react rapidly to news reports and, almost without exception, the change of government has occurred after weeks of rumours: in such cases, the change is not considered news and has already been priced into the markets.

But third, and most importantly, is the fact that no one is expecting significant policy changes. The forthcoming presidential and parliamentary (Duma) elections have created an environment where politicians are taking a cautious approach to economic policy and are doing as much as possible to do as little as possible. This has both positive and negative consequences: positive in that the policies have become predictable and any changes that would again severely damage the Russian economy look unlikely; but negative in that the political will to engage in the large-scale institutional and structural reforms essential to sustainable recovery is still absent (see Westin, 1999).

Once Russia recovers from campaign fever, a new president and Duma will have to face the underlying structural problems and lack of institutional development. The rest of this book discusses some of the most important issues and points to policy options. The fundamental challenge of rebuilding a constituency for implementing the necessary reforms remains.

2 Macroeconomic Policy and the Problem of Arrears

This chapter briefly surveys recent monetary, exchange rate and fiscal policy in Russia, drawing on *Russian Economic Trends* (see Westin, 1999), before focusing on the macroeconomics of arrears and research by Nadezhda Ivanova and Charles Wyplosz, presented at the RECEP conference.

The devaluation of the rouble on 17 August 1998 meant an end to the rouble corridor that had previously provided the foundation of Russia's monetary policy. Between August and October 1998, the rouble fell 150% in nominal terms; a depreciation of 80% in just seven weeks. Fearing further weakening of the rouble, and with insufficient international reserves, the CBR introduced a number of restrictions on trading and on current and capital account transactions.

As a rule, new restrictions like these have some short-term effect, but they are quickly circumvented so that depreciation is likely to resume. But the restriction on purchases of hard currency from correspondent accounts of foreign banks, introduced in April 1999, has had a more long-term stabilizing effect. The MICEX (Moscow Interbank Credit Exchange) exchange rate reached a record low of R27.40 to the dollar on 25 March, but since then, it has remained more or less stable at around R24. This means that a year after the crisis, the rouble had depreciated 25%.

In accordance with the IMF programme and the 'Memorandum of the Government of the Russian Federation and the Central Bank of Russia on Economic Policy', the exchange rate was unified at the end of June 1999. The special trading session for importers and exporters was scrapped, and trading returned to a unified session in line with Article VIII of the IMF charter, requiring a country to have a unified exchange rate. In addition, the restriction on foreign banks' correspondent accounts has been lifted. Worries were raised that when restrictions were lifted, the build-up of rouble liquidity at the CBR would swamp the currency market and drive the rouble down even further. This did not happen, although pressure has not been eliminated and the CBR has had to spend hundreds of millions of dollars to support the rouble.

Tight fiscal and monetary policy

A central cause of the August 1998 crisis was the dire state of Russia's budget. Years of large federal deficits financed by an unsustainable high-yielding pyramid-type treasury bills market brought Russia to the brink of financial collapse. One consequence of the crisis was the disappearance of securities markets as investor confidence dwindled, thus limiting the government's ability to finance the deficit.

Deprived of its main source of funding, the government was finally faced with no other alternative than to come up with a much tighter budget for 1999, foreseeing a primary surplus of 1.6% and a deficit after interest payments of 2.5%.

The government had struggled to fulfil its revenue target in previous years, but 1999 proved to be different (see Gorban and Westin, 1999, for a discussion of the draft 2000 budget). Not only has the government managed to meet and even exceed its targeted revenues, but more importantly, the bulk is now paid in cash. There are several explanations for this:

- First, the devaluation and continued depreciation of the rouble have resulted in higher rouble values of foreign trade taxes, which are set in hard currency; this is despite the contraction in imports by 45%.
- Second, the favourable conditions for exporters created by a weaker rouble and higher oil prices have allowed the government to collect higher revenues from export tariffs, especially from oil exports.
- Third, economic growth has not only created a wider tax base, but also improved the conditions for tax compliance.
- And finally, the government has been successful, both in managing to keep the VAT rate at 20%, and in its bargaining with energy sector enterprises, which have significantly increased cash payments to the budget.

Monetary policy has also remained relatively tight. In the year from August 1998 to August 1999, the monetary base increased by 63.3%, on average 4.1% per month. The bulk of the money printed has been used to meet external debt obligations but also to pay off budgetary wage arrears.

Large-scale indexation of wages and pensions has been avoided with a positive effect on inflation. It is true that consumer prices have increased by 120% August to August. But in September 1998, the monthly inflation rate was 38.4%, mainly an adjustment to the devaluation. Monthly inflation rates in the six months from February to August 1999 ranged between 1.2–3%. This is an impressive record, considering the predictions made in the immediate aftermath of the crisis. Nevertheless, two elections are scheduled in the next few months, and there is always a risk that expansionary monetary and fiscal policy decisions will be made in order to buy votes.

Arrears

From the beginning of the transition, the tide of arrears has been mounting relentlessly in Russia (see Ivanova and Wyplosz, 1998). Non-payments have been pervasive: from the state to its employees and providers of goods and services; from taxpayers to the state; and from firms to firms. The full extent of arrears is not known but it is remarkable how steady and widespread the increase in arrears has been. Ivanova and Wyplosz's research aims to shed some light on the mechanism of arrears growth and to assess the widely-held view that it is due to excessive monetary stringency.

It is clear that arrears accumulate in a vicious cycle. Firms that are owed payments by the government fail to pay taxes, pushing the government further into arrears.

The result is a complex web of linked debts. This has led to recurrent suggestions that all arrears should be consolidated and all debts undone in one big settlement. Several tax amnesties enacted in October 1993, January 1996 and March 1997 were efforts in this direction. Each time the stated intention was to trigger a virtuous cycle that would unravel the chain of non-payments.

Unfortunately, what happened was just the opposite: each amnesty was followed by another jump in tax arrears. It seems that non-compliant taxpayers have interpreted each amnesty as a promise of further forgiveness, and acted accordingly. In the same vein, the government has also offered to settle its own debts against tax arrears by offering so-called 'mutual offsets' on several occasions since March 1994. In fact, non-monetary offsets were continuously on offer from March 1994 to February 1998, when they were stopped in response to IMF pressure. But the idea of offset schemes has been revived since the crisis under the new name of 'targeted finance' – an attempt to repay government debt for goods and services supplied in 1997 and 1998. Offsets have been particularly large at the end of each year. Periods of large offsets coincide with a reduced flow of federal tax arrears, but the effect is only temporary and tax arrears promptly build up again.

It may seem surprising that the government is fully aware of its own contribution to the phenomenon yet has not eliminated the flow of its own arrears. There have been a few highly publicized attempts at 'cleaning up the desk', such as the drive to pay off salaries and pensions arrears in full by the end of 1997. But such initiatives have meant pulling resources from other budget commitments so that, in the end, overall government arrears did not decline.

One reason for the government's helplessness is the nature of the budget process, which is a lengthy trade-off between ministers and the Duma. The government acts strategically, submitting to the Duma a budget that it does not intend to execute. Estimates of spending on items the Duma is known to favour are deliberately underestimated by way of an initial bargaining position. The government draft also tends to set tax receipts lower than actually expected in an effort to discipline the Duma, which, in turn, acts strategically and forces adoption of a budget that is not workable. The result is a piece of legislation, usually adopted late, that has no credibility and is therefore ignored, at least in part, as the year unfolds. Actual revenues always fall short of the budget law while spending tends to be fully disbursed. What is missing in spending is 'financed' through arrears.

Over several years, the IMF has increasingly focused on the deficit as a key measure of Russia's adherence to its programme. Squeezed between the Duma and the IMF, with tax revenues declining as arrears to the budget rise, the government has responded by cutting spending and running arrears.

But the overall arrears situation in the Russian economy cannot be blamed only on the fiscal problems of the government. A major factor is the absence of the rule of law and a society that has no automatic penalty for non-payments. Creditors cannot put effective liens on debtors' assets, bankruptcies remain a rarity and firms can publicly report profits while not paying taxes and debts. In this context, arrears amount to free credit.

Arrears are sometimes seen as the market's spontaneous response to a key failure of the Russian economy, the virtual non-existence of bank credit. According to this view, firms use their workers and providers of intermediary products, including energy and other utilities, as implicit bankers because they have no access to proper credit. The opposite view is that causality runs in the opposite direction: banks do not grant commercial credit because widespread non-payments means that there can be no guarantee that the loans will be repaid and because collateral cannot be credibly pledged. In any case, implicitly borrowing from firms upstream in the production process is useless if partners downstream adopt the same behaviour; in the end, there can be no net credit, so that the result is a very inefficient outcome. Another possibility is that the government is used as residual lender.

Arrears are also a key reason for Russia's lacklustre economic performance since 1991. The absence of commercial credit undermines proper allocation of savings, and prevents a new private sector from emerging, vigorously in opposition to the restructured former state sector. Arrears further encourage the development of barter trade and non-cash payments of taxes. Another market response to non-payments and the absence of commercial credit is the creation of large holdings, within which payment discipline is imposed and resources can circulate. These holdings come to dominate the economy and the polity, blocking reforms that would undermine their very reasons to exist.

Policy implications

It is not surprising that the debate on arrears remains murky. Popular explanations include a cash drought (blamed on the CBR), the end of subsidies to ailing corporations, and budgetary tightness. Ivanova and Wyplosz's research attempts to detect such macroeconomic factors, focusing on tax arrears – non-payments to the federal government. While the available evidence is limited, and the shortness of the time series a problem, they are able to draw the following conclusions:

- First, all forms of arrears appear to be linked and to respond to a common causal factor. Enterprises under duress run arrears, first to the budget, and then to other enterprises and to their own employees. This ranking follows the line of least resistance. It is clearly less dangerous to upset the tax collector than to upset colleagues or employees.
- Second, there is indirect evidence that non-payment of taxes reflects long-term corporate distress rather than temporary difficulties. That observation suggests that the arrears phenomenon is a feature associated with the fact that large segments of Russian industry have not yet been restructured. Put differently, an acceleration of the pace of industry-level reform is likely to reduce arrears to the budget and not to increase them, despite claims to the contrary.
- Third, arrears result from the balance of two costs: the opportunity cost of borrowing and the implicit expected cost of non-compliance. Both operate through the real interest rate. It is not possible to separate the operation of these two effects, although some clues can be found in the following points.
- Fourth, the role of monetary policy is not clear-cut. Higher real interest rates increase arrears but so does an increase in the real money supply. Causation between real money and increases in arrears runs both ways (after 1994) with two widely different interpretations. It may be that tight money hurts firms or

it may be that firms run arrears to accumulate money because it is profitable to do so.
- Fifth, fiscal policy tightness increases arrears if it takes the form of a reduction in expenditures, though the effect is relatively small. On the other side of the budget, reductions in tax collection do not affect arrears.
- Sixth, taken together, the two previous observations indicate that tight macroeconomic policies may contribute to increasing arrears. This does not mean that fiscal and monetary policies should be relaxed for the sake of dealing with arrears. Macroeconomic policies ought to be set according to macroeconomic objectives, but it is important to be aware of the implication for arrears.
- Seventh, tax amnesties reduce the cost of non-compliance and directly raise the level of arrears.
- Eighth, by contrast, a tough approach to arrears works. Bankrupting firms that do not pay taxes is likely to be the most powerful tool for combating arrears to the budget. After all, that is how it is done elsewhere in the world!

3 Tax Collection and Fiscal Federalism

This chapter summarizes research on the fiscal crisis in Russia, the country's tax capacity and its tax collection performance relative to that capacity, and the intergovernmental organization of the budgetary system – what is known as fiscal federalism. The work was presented at the RECEP conference in papers by Rory MacFarquhar and Katherina Zhuravskaya (see MacFarquhar, 1998, and Zhuravskaya, 1998, 1999).

Can't tax or won't tax?

Russia's legendary failure to collect taxes is frequently cited as the most glaring sign of the weakness of the Russian state. Few analyses of the financial crisis of August 1998 have failed to mention Russia's deficient tax system as a key cause of the collapse. Revenue-raising measures have dominated the government's discussions with the IMF for the last few years, and on several occasions, loan tranches were withheld to punish Russia for failing to meet tax collection targets.

But, MacFarquhar asks, does Russia really collect an unusually small amount in taxes? His research seeks to identify a 'steady state' level for Russia's budget using broad international comparisons. The results show that Russia is close to the level that would be expected of a country of its size, income and economic structure. Tax evasion and arrears are certainly rampant, but it seems that they should be understood as the result of the state's attempt to extract more from the private sector than is feasible for a country in Russia's position.

MacFarquhar argues that explanations for the fiscal crisis should be sought in the level of expenditure and the distribution of revenues among levels of government rather than in the performance of the tax system. An important cause of the federal government's default in August 1998 was an outflow of revenues from the federal budget to the regions. Conversely, in the first half of 1999, revenue performance at the federal level improved dramatically, largely at the expense of the regions.

The fiscal crisis

As in all transition countries, Russia suffered a sharp decline in government revenue in the early years of transition. Between 1992–5, general government revenues (including federal, regional, local and off-budget revenues) fell from 44% of GDP

– the share collected by many Western European countries – to 34% of GDP, or about the share collected by Japan and the United States. Since 1994, general government revenues have remained fairly stable in the range of 32–35% of GDP. Over the same period, however, the Russian economy shrank by a half, more than proportionally contracting the bases of many taxes. Moreover, privatization moved over 70% of value added from state ownership at least nominally into the private sector; in principle, the scaling back of state responsibilities should reduce the demand for government spending.

Russia's fiscal authorities at all levels of government signally failed to adjust to the new reality of reduced spending possibilities. At the federal level, each annual budget law pledged to raise more revenue than the previous year, and increased spending accordingly. Political confrontation with a hostile Duma ensured that budgets were passed with delays and were consistently unrealistic. Each year, revenues fell short of the budget target. The result was an unbroken string of large federal budget deficits over the course of a decade. Between 1992–4, the federal government financed its deficits by printing money; thereafter, it relied on GKOs, a third of which were owned by foreigners by 1998. At the same time, the government borrowed heavily abroad: in the 10 years leading up to the crisis, the Soviet Union's, and subsequently Russia's, foreign debt quadrupled, as successive governments borrowed over $100 billion from foreign governments, banks and international financial institutions.

In addition to the explicit, securitized debt, the federal government accumulated large, poorly documented wage and payment arrears to its employees and suppliers. Limits on the availability of financing and pressure from the IMF led the government to make arbitrary spending cuts in order to contain the cash deficit. But policy disagreements within the government, lobbying by self-interested banks, and a dubious emphasis on 'state secrecy' in the extensive security apparatus all prevented the state treasury from taking control of the spending commitments by line ministries.

As a result, the only way the Ministry of Finance could contain the deficit was to withhold cash payments. It estimated that these arrears had reached R60 billion (2% of GDP) by 1997, six times the official figure. Roughly two thirds of the arrears were cleared in the 'reverse offset' scheme between November 1997 and February 1998, but arrears returned in 1998 as the Ministry of Finance cut discretionary spending to cover the rising costs of debt service. Weak spending controls also gave line ministries and regional governments a strategic incentive to bargain for an increase in their total allocation by spending on unbudgeted discretionary projects while running up arrears on necessities, such as wages – a phenomenon well-known in other parts of the world.

Over the same period, regional governments and off-budget funds were able to take an increasing share of general government revenues. In 1992, the federal government collected 36% of general government revenues, not including the inflation tax, which also accrued primarily to the federal government. By 1998, after a short recovery in 1995, its share had fallen by almost a third to 26% of the total.

Regions increased their share partly through political bargaining over transfers and revenue-sharing agreements with the federal government and partly by seizing more revenue than their legal entitlement. There is some controversy over the extent to which regions have been able to withhold federal revenue through direct intervention, but regions have also found indirect ways of increasing their share of total revenues. Most significant among those is the acceptance of payment in the form of barter and mutual clearing operations, which the regions have relied on to a greater extent than has the federal government. State tax service data indicate that on average only 50% of regional taxes were in money in 1997, compared to 65% of federal revenues.

Not only did this fiscal decentralization leave the federal government unable to pay its debts, but it also undermined many of the priorities of reform. When the federal government attempted to force companies to restructure by reducing subsidies, regional governments took over. As much as 40% of regional spending in 1996 and 1997 (6.5% of GDP) was allocated to various forms of industrial, agricultural and housing subsidies. At the same time, the regional governments ran up public sector wage arrears in a bid to extract additional resources from the centre, and the federal government was repeatedly forced to oblige them.

A striking feature of the post-crisis fiscal recovery is the resurgence of federal revenue at the expense of the regions. General government revenues in the first half of 1999 are slightly up from the previous year, though they remain below the 1997 level. But the federal budget's share of general government revenues (after transfers) rose from 26% in 1997 and 1998 to 32% in the first half of 1999, while the share accruing to regional and local budgets fell by an equal amount. The shift was the result less of deliberate policy than of changing economic circumstances: the federal government benefited more than the regions from buoyant revenues from exports and from higher world commodity prices.

Russia's tax capacity

Since 1994, Russia's general government revenues have remained remarkably stable as a share of GDP, despite variations in government personnel (including five prime ministers, eight finance ministers and five heads of the state tax service), political circumstances (two elections and two wars), financial market conditions, tax legislation and IMF pressure. This stability-amid-flux suggests that Russia may be facing economic constraints on its ability to tax rather than suffering from a lack of political 'will'. MacFarquhar's research seeks to obtain predictions for how much Russia can expect to raise in taxes.

In the 1960s and 1970s, economists at the IMF and elsewhere started estimating taxable capacity using cross-country data. They then assessed each country's 'tax effort' – that is, how hard the government tried to collect taxes – as the ratio of taxes actually collected to the amount predicted by their simple model. This literature has been much criticized for its attempts to make normative claims based on comparisons of actual tax systems and for its assumption that cross-sectional comparisons necessarily have implications for individual countries' development over time. Moreover, in these models, it is not necessarily possible to distinguish determinants of tax capacity from determinants of tax effort. Nonetheless, the approach represents a significant advance over international comparisons of tax ratios, and draws attention to important factors that affect countries' ability and willingness to extract revenues for public purposes.

The literature identifies several economic variables as bearing on a country's taxable capacity:

- The most common is per capita GDP. When the population is richer, there is a larger 'surplus' available to be taxed. Higher income also accompanies higher levels of education, which affects people's willingness to pay taxes voluntarily. Higher per capita income may also affect people's preference for government services: the 'Wagner hypothesis' states that government services are a luxury good, the demand for which should rise disproportionately with income.
- A second variable commonly used to predict taxable capacity is the share of value added produced in agriculture. The agricultural sector is notoriously difficult to tax, partly because, in developing countries, subsistence agriculture has only occasional contact with the money economy. Thus, a higher agricultural share in GDP should lead to lower revenue collection.
- Openness to foreign trade has been shown to lead to higher revenues, both because border crossings are the easiest place to collect revenues and because a high level of foreign trade is an indicator of more sophisticated markets and a money-based economy.
- Production of natural resources, particularly fossil fuels, is thought to increase taxable capacity, since hydrocarbons are usually mined by a few readily identifiable firms generating a relatively large taxable surplus.
- Finally, it is worth estimating the effect of monetization of the economy on revenue collection directly. It could be expected that a smaller money supply indicates prevalence of non-monetary forms of exchange, or pervasive capital flight, both of which make tax collection more difficult.

MacFarquhar's calculations of Russia's tax capacity reveal that, contrary to the conventional wisdom, Russia collects about as much in taxes as would be expected for a country of its income and economic structure, based on international comparisons. Based on the 49 developed, developing and transition countries for which data are available, Russia is predicted to collect 32–33% of GDP, compared with an actual value of 33% of GDP.

Taking account of Russia's federal structure reduces the predicted value to 28% of GDP. Only when a dummy variable is included for transition countries is the predicted value higher than the current actual level, 38% of GDP. When the model is evaluated for non-transition countries, it yields a predicted value of 24% of GDP for Russia. So, were Russia an average market economy of its income and structure, it would be collecting a quarter less in revenue than it is at present.

The economic collapse of the 1990s and the liberalization of the economy has severely limited the state's ability to extract revenue. Indeed, the recent rebound in revenue at the federal level has come largely at the expense of regional and local budgets: general government revenues in the first half of 1999 remain lower than in 1997.

MacFarquhar concludes that only sustained economic recovery will restore Russia's tax capacity. Meanwhile, the government must scale back its ambitions and begin to live within its means. Otherwise, continuing macroeconomic instability will delay that recovery even further.

Inter-governmental relations

In recent years, economists have increasingly stressed the idea that good economic institutions, including those in the public sector, are instrumental for economic growth. One of the most important of these institutions in a federation is fiscal federalism. According to Katherina Zhuravskaya, inefficient inter-governmental relations may be an important reason for Russia's poor growth performance.

Ideally, fiscal federalism should promote territorial justice, economic efficiency and political stability. These goals are often contradictory, but the idea is to find the least costly compromise. Analysis of Russia's system of inter-governmental relations shows that the country is still very far from having implemented these principles. From the economist's point of view, the most important criterion for the organization of inter-governmental relations is that it must create incentives for economic development and investment in infrastructure. The main underlying principles of 'market preserving' federalism are as follows:

- Equality of all regions in their budget relations with the federal centre and of all localities in their relations with the regional centre. No discrimination either for or against certain regions or localities should be allowed.
- Independence of budgets of different tiers that includes: own sources of income for each level, fixed by legislation; the right to decide on own composition of expenditures; the impossibility of taxing away additional revenues by the upper level of government; the right to be compensated for additional mandatory expenditures that appeared because of legislative amendments of the upper levels of government; and the right to give any tax breaks that would affect only own sources of revenue.
- Legally established (fixed and transparent) distribution of expenditure responsibilities and sources of revenues between different levels of government. The principles of revenue sharing may be crucial for creating growth incentives.
- Correspondence of the expenditure responsibilities at every level of government with own revenues at that level.
- Any redistribution of financial resources between the subjects of the federation or localities in one region, or financial aid to another level of government should follow objective criteria, be transparent and have a long-term legal basis; that is, not subject to any bargaining.
- All disputes about tax revenues or budgetary process should be solved according to law-based standards.

The incentives created by Russian fiscal federalism have been extensively studied. Credit for the study of federal–regional relations goes mainly to Daniel Treisman (1996) and Alexey Lavrov (1996) while Zhuravskaya's work on local government incentives has shed light on the economics of sub-regional relations, relations between provinces or republics and their constitutive districts (see Zhuravskaya, 1998). These studies suggest that the term 'fiscal federalism' definitely needs to be put in quotes when applied to Russia.

Federal–regional relations

Over the last decade, the federal government has signed bilateral treaties with different subjects of the federation that individually regulate its relationships with the regions. The terms of these treaties vary substantially, which creates a confusing and non-transparent system. The division of power and responsibilities between different levels of government is specified by law in a very vague fashion, especially at the sub-regional level. In general, sub-federal (local) governments are responsible for provision of the most important and inelastic expenditures such as health, education and housing subsidies, while the most inelastic revenues accrue to the centre. This mismatch creates a need for an unreasonable amount of fiscal redistribution and it has intensified the payments crisis, income disparities and emergence of administrative controls over inter-regional trade and mobility of people and capital.

Fiscal redistribution between the regions takes place on a large scale. But it has never been transparent or followed pre-set rules. Horse trading over federal transfers has created a system with perverse incentives for inefficient spending and poor tax collection by regions. According to Treisman, neither low ability to pay for public services, implementation of economic reform (so that policy is aligned with the policy chosen by the centre) nor efficiency in tax collection tend to earn a region a larger net transfer. In fact, the reverse often seems to be the case. Regional expressions of political discontent (such as anti-reform voting or a governor publicly opposing President Yeltsin) seem to elicit outbursts of placatory generosity from the centre.

While redistribution favours big spenders and currently unprofitable regions over their frugal and efficient neighbours, it does not seem to channel transfers to regions with the poorest provision of social infrastructure, judged by past revenues and spending. The transfers have generally not been equalizing either, since in several years the dispersion of regional budgetary funds per capita before transfers was smaller than after transfers. Almost any transparent formula based on objective criteria would improve incentives in the regions if implemented. Unfortunately, the centre has been politically unable to commit to a set rule for redistribution.

Sub-regional relations

The main underlying principle of fiscal federalism – independence of different tiers of government – has been harshly violated at the sub-regional level as well. Local governments in big donor-cities have been unable to benefit from an increase in their local tax base because any increase in their tax revenues is immediately followed by an equal decrease in federal transfers to the region, where the city is located, or in the share of regional taxes that go to the city budget. Moreover, local governments that experience decreases in budget revenues have been bailed out by regional administrations.

This system encourages poor tax collection and attempts by local administrations to use barter tax collection and non-transparent off-budget funds in an attempt to protect their own revenues from confiscation. The enormous scale of economically unjustified political intervention in business by local administrations, including excessive regulation and subsidies to large inefficient enterprises, could also be explained by the lack of fiscal incentives to support efficient business. In a system where local governments can keep their own revenues, there would probably be smaller subsidies, more benign regulation and higher growth compared to what happens in Russia.

In sum, the Russian system of inter-governmental relations gives incentives to government officials at all levels for poor tax collection, rebellion against the federal centre (in the case of regions) and against the region (in the case of localities), and for inefficient overspending and subsidies. Lack of clarity in the division of revenue and expenditure responsibilities leads to constant bargaining between regions and the federation.

The main finding of Zhuravskaya's research on sub-federal relations is that localities never became independent from the regional governments. Local officials have not been given sufficient responsibility for their decisions on expenditures and have not been granted the right to raise their own revenues. Her work provides evidence that revenue-sharing relations between local and regional governments hinder local government's incentives to provide infrastructure for private business development. In addition, it shows that the fiscal dependence of local governments affects the distribution of public spending over different budget items and has a negative effect on the efficiency of local public goods provision. Therefore, economic reform needs to be supported by the reform of government institutions.

Policy implications

Zhuravskaya concludes that a federal law is needed that would clearly regulate the redistribution process between the federation and regions and localities. On both the federal and sub-federal levels, funds should be distributed according to a fixed, long-term formula based on objective criteria. What is more, the division of tax revenues should be hard and fast, and there should be no room for renegotiation of these arrangements. Regions could themselves design the rules for redistribution between localities. The most important criterion for such rules should be that local tax revenues will not be redistributed in a confiscatory manner, thus leaving incentives for efficient tax collection and fostering the local tax base.

These transparent, clearly defined, long-term rules for fiscal redistribution should be made simple (even at the cost of some efficiency loss), because simple rules are much easier to implement. How to prevent the federal and regional centres from taxing away additional revenues of the lower levels of government is a difficult problem, but an open and transparent system should help.

Distribution of expenditure responsibilities between the different tiers also needs to be much better defined. Most of all, the distribution of expenditure responsibilities between regional and local governments needs much improvement since mandatory shifts of expenditures from regional to local governments often occur without a required transfer of funds to finance these additional expenditures.

Openness of the budgetary system is also vital for making election mechanisms work properly. Taxpayers and voters need to know where their money is spent, so that they can vote an inefficient manager of public money out of office. There also needs to be much better control over distribution of federal funds to the regions to combat misuse of money at the regional level. There are four main things that could be done here:

- All federal expenditures with no exceptions should be made through the treasury system for better control over the use of budget funds. Strengthening of the treasury system in all ministries and regions is the only way for the federal government to control expenditures and ultimately reduce government arrears.
- Federal government should take over revenues from budgetary funds, which have the highest incidence of misuses of funds due to their lack of transparency. The resources of the road fund alone (R13 billion for first half of 1998) would be sufficient to cover public wage arrears.
- Making all federal transfers targeted (that is, earmarked for specific kinds of expenditure) would improve the ability of the centre to control the use of funds.
- Federal transfers to the localities should be made directly to the localities and not via regions. Much of the money from the federal fund for support of subjects of the federation is reallocated by the regions to the localities. It would be better to transfer money directly to the localities from the federal budget in order to reduce the misuse of funds on the regional level.

In recent years, there has been a weakening of the already weak tax base for the localities, increasing the dependence of localities on the regions. The localities should be given additional sources for their own revenues. And overall, the federal government should demonstrate its credibility in implementing the policy of tax discipline by bankrupting large non-payers and repossessing their assets, and following pre-set rules on distributions of transfer.

4 Banking and the Financial–Industrial Groups

This chapter briefly surveys Russia's banking crisis, the role of the so-called Financial–Industrial Groups (FIGs), and a possible strategy for bank restructuring. It draws primarily on research by Enrico Perotti, some of which was presented at the RECEP conference, as well as work by David Brown and colleagues published in *Russian Economic Trends* (see Perotti, 1999a,b; Perotti and Gelfer, 1998; Brown et al., 1999).

The banking crisis

The August 1998 devaluation and default on the government's domestic debt was followed by the collapse of the Russian banking sector. By the end of the month, almost half of the commercial banks, including the state-owned savings bank, Sberbank, were experiencing enormous problems in meeting their obligations. The payment system began to fall apart and many people were refused access to their savings.

The banking crisis revealed the extreme vulnerability and shakiness of Russian credit institutions. The biggest single reason for the breakdown of the banking system was the assumption by Russian bankers that the state would act as creditor of last resort and even as a guarantor of the stability of their institutions. Counting on the softness of the budget constraint they were facing, many of the banks took large credits from foreign investors in 1997 when Russia's popularity on international markets was at its peak and interest rates on such loans were not very high.

Banks often channelled these credits into risky and inefficient projects. Although CBR figures put the value of bad loans on the books of Russian banks in 1997 at just 11% of total bank credit to the private sector, anecdotal evidence suggests that the real figures were much higher. Some estimates put the volume of bad loans as high as 75% of total lending by banks to the private sector.

In addition, the banks were heavily invested in government and commercial paper, the value of which plummeted with the stock market crash and the debt default. The rouble's fall meant that these assets shrank further in relation to the banks' dollar liabilities. The situation was further aggravated by a large number of forward contracts into which many banks had entered, committing themselves to sell hard currency to counterparties at an agreed rate on an agreed future date – and hence leaving themselves heavily exposed to rouble risk.

The emergence of FIGs

Related to the problems in the banking sector was the emergence of the FIGs (see Perotti, 1999a). These groups involve close relationships between financial institutions and industrial enterprises to a degree not observed in mature market economies, where firms access capital primarily via arm's-length contracting with institutions and capital markets. Many Russian FIGs have been built around one of the big and politically influential Moscow banks, which, thanks to powerful connections, managed to acquire large controlling stakes in enterprises during the privatization process.

The political power held by the FIGs played an important role in the process that caused the crisis. They offered a convenient route for tax evasion and capital flight via under-invoicing for exports and over-invoicing for imports. Their control over media and finance has also reinforced their political power and, hence, their ability to influence or even blackmail the government in a pattern typical of corporate groups in many developing countries. The recklessness of many banks' practices and the credibility granted to them, for a time, by foreign investors can only be understood in terms of easy access to political and financial favours.

There is much debate about the benefits and dangers of consolidation of companies and financial institutions into conglomerates, *keiretsu*, *chaebols* and FIGs. West Germany and Japan relied on such structures to rebuild their post-war economies. In the 1960s, similar entities appeared in the less developed countries of South East Asia and Latin America, and now they have emerged in the former Soviet bloc countries, notably in Russia. Until recently, many believed that the exceptional growth of the Asian economies such as Japan and Korea showed that these structures can be a successful organizational alternative to the traditional corporate structures of Western economies. But there is increasing scepticism about their efficiency, as the crises in the Asian economies and in Russia cast a shadow over the benefits of agglomeration.

Roles of FIGs

Financial–Industrial Groups and similar conglomerates have a tendency to appear in countries where capital is scarce. In such environments they can play a number of roles.

Increasing the productivity of capital where legal institutions are weak

One of the main spurs towards formation of FIGs has been the failure of the authorities to protect property rights. This was the case in many Asian countries, and is still the case in Russia, where the court system is very weak, and bankruptcy laws favour debtors and are not easily enforceable. In such an environment, FIGs can offer a safe haven where property rights are enforced and contracts are honoured: capital holders have chosen to own or financially control the companies in which they are investing so that they can monitor and enforce repayment of credits without resorting to court measures. In addition, firms that are grouped together by cross ownership and/or a technological chain may have more incentives to make relationship-specific investments and less incentives to renege on their contracts with each other because they are confident of the long-term nature of their relationship.

Substituting for missing or highly imperfect capital markets

Capital markets in many developing and transition economies are rudimentary. Equity markets are illiquid and banking systems are weak. Inefficient corporate governance and monitoring systems intensify informational asymmetry between borrowers and creditors. Diversified conglomerates, which tie together industry and finance, can provide services that are absent or ineffective in emerging markets, such as venture capital investments, private equity provision, mutual funds and banking. For example, a FIG can use internally-generated resources and invest them in existing or new businesses. Banks, which lend to firms in which they hold substantial equity stakes, have an incentive to monitor the firms, thereby reducing the agency costs of debt and providing a more attractive investment proposition for other domestic lenders and for foreign capital. In Russia, with its young and inexperienced banking system, the non-existence of commercial debt markets and an under-capitalized stock market, the situation begged for the creation of some alternative mechanism to finance real sector projects.

Improving production performance through economies of scale

In emerging markets, there is often a scarcity of well-trained management. FIGs can substitute for such institutions as head-hunting agencies, relocation services and management institutes, which exist in developed economies. Large business groups can incur the fixed costs of setting up infrastructure to develop management talent. Dissemination of information about new technology and know-how is facilitated when the information flows freely across the firms that are grouped in a FIG. Integration also provides a risk-spreading mechanism in the face of firm-specific and sector-specific shocks, smoothing out the income streams for the group as a whole. There is evidence of such economies of scale in several studies of Indian, Korean and Japanese firms.

Minimizing price distortions resulting from state interference in markets

Emerging markets are often characterized by complex regulatory intervention by government, leading to a lack of transparency in the rules that govern business interaction with government. In Russia, the state sector is still very large by international standards and Russian small firms report much higher licensing, tax and registration costs than those in other transition economies (see Johnson et al., 1998). FIGs can forge strong relationships with bureaucrats, so that regulations are interpreted and executed in a way that favours the FIG or specific companies within it. Extensive business–government relationships exist in many emerging markets, but these relationships can become a serious burden on the economy when they are allowed to flourish.

The drawbacks of a FIG-dominated economy

The main drawback of agglomeration is that it often leads to the concentration of economic and political power in the hands of a few businessmen, in Russia's case, the 'oligarchs'. By exploiting such power, FIGs slow down the restructuring of the country's enterprises, create fragility in the banking system and contribute to the economic crisis.

As FIGs become large, they can acquire significant bargaining power in their relationship with the state. It is usually politically difficult for a government to allow bankruptcy of a large conglomerate that employs many people and has obligations to a large number of foreign and domestic savers. Therefore, a bankruptcy threat is often not credible for a FIG and, as a result, its directors have fewer incentives than the managers of small enterprises to operate efficiently. The softness of the budget constraint can be manifested in many ways, ranging from subsidies to FIG enterprises and tolerance of FIG tax arrears (particularly widespread in Russia) to bailouts of bankrupt FIG banks. Other favours include cheap credits and import barriers.

The presence of soft budget constraints usually leads to many inefficiencies, including:

- So-called 'socialist' lending inside FIGs, which allocates lending on other criteria than expected returns from projects. This leads to a large number of bank loans and to under-financing of worthy projects.
- Overleveraging of FIGs, which are perceived as 'too big too fail' by investors, and, therefore, can attract large amounts of capital. Korea was a striking example of this: *chaebols*, which promoted the country's growth when they were first formed, had grown very big by the mid-1990s and become heavily indebted. The debt to equity ratio for the top 30 *chaebols* stood at 400%. Many of these loans were from abroad, and when at the end of 1997, Korea was forced to devalue its currency, the financial system of the country collapsed.
- Excessive risk-taking by the financial components of a FIG.
- Asset stripping of companies inside the group.

Although FIGs do contribute to growth in the early stages of their development, they can eventually lead to inefficiencies by promoting too close a relationship between businesses, banks and the government throughout the economy. Countries where government involvement in the system was minimal were able to move away from these structures once they became sub-optimal. In other economies, the relationship with the state insulated member firms from market forces. Exacerbated by a lack of transparency and accountability in the business groups, government patronage led to the perpetuation of existing inefficiencies, which made the economy very vulnerable to external shocks. The period 1997–8 demonstrated this admirably in Korea, Thailand and Russia, as the emerging market crisis swept the globe.

FIG membership and economic performance

Research by David Brown and colleagues, published in *Russian Economic Trends*, explores whether being a member of an official (registered) or informal FIG makes a difference for an industrial firm. They find that membership of groups is significant for the economic performance of firms, and this is true not only for informal FIGs, but also for official FIGs. Groups are good for their members: they offer better access to credit, and they help to increase labour productivity and exports. But FIGs hurt independent firms: wherever groups are prevalent, new entry into product markets is lower.

The benefits of group membership vary between official and informal FIGs. The impact on access to credit markets and on exports is larger for informal FIGs, whereas only official FIGs appear to have the effect of foreclosing markets. Credit market access and exports may be more important for both types of FIGs than vertical and horizontal integration, since membership of conglomerate groups has the largest effect on labour productivity.

Policy-makers should take these advantages and disadvantages of FIGs into account. So far, the Russian government has preferred to allow and even encourage the growth of these groups. This may well have been justified given the advantages they provided for their members. But it is vital to bear in mind that FIGs have a negative effect on competition and flexibility, both of which are crucial for long-term growth.

Restructuring Russia's banks

Despite various reform proposals, the collapse of the Russian banking sector in August 1998 has barely been addressed and numerous problems remain. Citizens' confidence in banks remains extremely low: CBR data indicates that there was a net outflow of household deposits from commercial banks between September 1998 and January 1999 towards cash and Sberbank, with commercial banks' volume falling by 18%. It is essential to bring domestic private savings back into the financial system to reduce interest rates and fund restructuring as well as the state budget.

The trouble is that there are far too many insolvent banks, which destroy the reputation of the solvent banks and discourage a return to rouble deposits. Bankers have few incentives to follow prudential investment strategies and remain solvent: there are few good assets and too many banks, so most of them prefer speculation or asset stripping. The monitoring capacity of the CBR is overwhelmed by the number of insolvent banks. Its task must be simplified by creating safe banks (which can only invest in safe assets) and reducing the number of active commercial banks.

Foreign assistance will depend on a clear bank restructuring programme that indicates what form the banking system will take in the medium term and why it may give better guarantees of solvency. But such assistance will be insufficient to recapitalize any of the current large banks.

According to Enrico Perotti, the collapse of the Russian financial system and the virtual bankruptcy of its banking system has not resulted in a policy response commensurate with the scale of the crisis. He argues for a strategy of 'jump-starting' bank restructuring. Given the rapid dissipation of assets in the banking sector, there is scope in this sector to create a market structure *ex novo*. What Perotti proposes is a crude solution based on a recognition of the impossibility of reliable supervision and contractual certainty in the short term (see Perotti, 1999b). The goals of the strategy are as follows:

- To obtain support from a sufficient number of large players to unblock reforms.
- To create a safe layer to restart basic banking services and re-intermediate savings.
- To create incentives for less risk-taking in banking.
- To create *ex post* incentives for a tough bankruptcy policy for insolvent banks, which does not require much administrative capacity or careful monitoring.

Perotti's proposed strategy has three ingredients. The first is the establishment of a narrow bank sector that will ensure a country-wide retail operation network and the essential core payment system. Only in this sector would deposits be insured, and then only partially. This provision will provide competition for the *de facto* monopolization of the retail sector under Sberbank, which is the sole insured bank. Licensing new banks to take over the retail and payment transfer facilities of failed banks should provide competition for Sberbank. The limited funds available to ARCO, the new agency that has been announced to deal with bank restructuring, should be used for this purpose.

Narrow banks would be able to invest only in safe assets, mostly government and CBR liabilities. But, while narrow banking is sometimes thought to limit the extent of risk-taking and financial panics, what happens is that risky activities are simply shifted elsewhere. The second ingredient of Perotti's strategy is therefore the sequential closure of over 90% of all banks and the creation of a *de facto* concentrated commercial banking segment, to be achieved via an extremely strict bank licensing. To restore some assets to the pilfered institutions and the bank restructuring authorities, such banks may emerge from already existing banks, formally liquidated and then resold under condition of proper recapitalization. Conceivably, some flight capital may return for this purpose.

The small number of banks remaining should have two implications: first, supervision will be viable even under the limited financial and technical resources of the CBR. Second, and far more importantly, there will be a powerful incentive created by establishing oligopolistic rents on which control rights are allocated *ex ante*. This high 'charter' value of a banking licence would restore incentives for bankers to focus on lower risk strategies.

Obviously, the licensing mechanism will succeed only if there is a steady supervision of the few banks allowed and a pre-emptive review cycle. There has to be a credible exit route, meaning that the banking regulator will have to resist any political opposition to a bank closure. On the other hand, if the rules of engagement are that a bank in trouble will be forced to sell shares to new shareholders, this would mean a serious loss of valuable control over the banking licence and strong incentives for other bankers to support enforcement. In an oligopolistic market, there is less potential for a united front of bankers if there are clear guidelines for reselling assets to banks that remain solvent. Currently, the opposite is true: all bankers share a common interest in stopping any legislation that will make easier to close down banks.

The last, essential and possibly most vulnerable part of Perotti's proposed strategy is the creation of a more transparent bank supervisory institution. This institution must be able to impose asset freezes and force shareholders to dilute their control through recapitalization via new share issues well ahead of financial distress. This arrangement is critical to ensuring an exit route and an ultimate source of discipline.

The institutional design must stress transparency and there is a strong argument to give significant powers to ARCO to counterbalance the CBR's powers.

In some ways, the proposed strategy parallels Russia's mass privatization programme and this suggests certain risks. Privatization was a remarkable achievement even in its general failure to induce rapid restructuring. The arrangement succeeded in overcoming enormous political and economic opposition because it recognized that private property rights were shattered and dispersed in Russia; that various players held partial control rights and thus could oppose and block privatization; and that these players had to be bought off with part of the spoils. The problem was that the process was captured too soon and produced an insider-dominated, cashless firm structure hostile (or not credible) to investors. Similar risks exist here.

But while efforts at institution-building and legal and contractual education are important, what is needed now are not better rules but sustainable rules of engagement, which will reverse the perverse incentives in the financial system to maximize risk-taking and eventually to socialize losses and abscond with the profits. The destruction of even the most elementary deposit or intermediation arrangements is a tremendous cost for a country with a complex economic structure and steep financial needs in both the short and medium term.

5 Industrial Restructuring

This chapter focuses on two important issues relating to Russian industry, both of which were discussed at the RECEP conference. One is the impact of market structure on competition and industrial performance, at both a national and regional level (see Brown and Brown, 1998); the other is what kind of industrial policy might be desirable in Russia so as to encourage much-needed enterprise restructuring (see Grosfeld and Senik-Leygonie, 1998).

Does market structure matter?

Annette Brown and David Brown's research addresses a long-standing question in economics: whether market structure – simply defined as the size and number of firms in an industry – affects competition between firms and thus the prices and output in that industry. Many economic models as well as observations of real economies suggest that if a market is dominated by one or a few large firms, those firms will have market power, allowing them to make higher profits at the expense of consumers. Frequently, governments use measures of market structure or concentration to inform pro-competition policies. But more recent models suggest that firms in concentrated markets may behave as if they are in competitive markets. Examples support these theories too.

For decades, economists have addressed this question using inter-industry data on concentration and profit margins. Some find a clear positive relationship between market concentration and profitability; others find no relationship; while still others find a clear negative relationship. There are two problems with these studies: first, it is difficult to test for a causal relationship between two factors that are both outcomes of market forces and clearly influence one another. In other words, market concentration is *endogenous* to industry profitability in market economies, making it difficult to test for the causal impact of concentration on profitability. The second problem is that data have been limited: governments publish only one or two measures of concentration and these are almost always calculated at the national level. So, using these data to represent market concentration implies that competition in every market occurs at the national level.

Russia's economic transition offers a unique opportunity to re-examine the question: its industrial structure at the beginning of transition was the structure inherited from the Soviets, and was thus *exogenous* to market forces and market-determined profitability. During the Soviet period, central planners together with government ministers determined industry structure according to various objectives. Even to the extent that cost minimization was one of those objectives, planners' cost estimates were based on relative prices that were unconnected to market prices. So markets clearly did not determine the industrial structure in Soviet Russia.

Brown and Brown's first analysis of the relationship between market structure and profitability in Russia suggests that concentration has no effect on industry profitability, no matter how concentration is measured. Their estimates support the view that the positive relationship found in earlier studies arises due to the endogeneity of market structure and not because concentration has a causal impact on profitability. But these results alone do not prove the theory wrong. The absence of a relationship in the basic model could be because of a mismeasurement of market concentration caused by improper definition of markets. If the market relevant for the competition facing a firm is smaller than the national market, then nationally-measured concentration measures alone are insufficient to test the relationship between concentration and profitability.

To correct for this problem, Brown and Brown introduce a measure of geographical dispersion. In theory, the spatial dispersion of production can affect profitability in several ways. Generally, economists hypothesize that dispersion decreases competition and should lead to greater industry profitability. More specifically, though, high degrees of dispersion probably reflect industries where markets are local or regional rather than national. In these cases, the national measure of concentration alone is a meaningless measure of competition. Oligopoly theory also suggests that clustering may have an effect on competition and profitability for firms in an oligopolistic industry. For example, suppose there are two firms in the same industry and they are both currently charging the same high price. If they are located near one another, each firm is less likely to undercut its rival because the rival will detect the price cut immediately and match it, causing both firms to lose profits.

Including dispersion in their model, Brown and Brown find that the interaction between dispersion and concentration has a positive effect on profitability. This result means that industries that are nationally concentrated – which have few firms or are dominated by a few firms – and that are geographically dispersed – the firms are all located in different localities – have higher profitability. The interpretation is that each of these firms acts like a monopoly in its local or regional market and is not threatened by competition from other firms in the industry. Since the other firms are few, each has its own market. In other words, the higher profitability comes from firms having monopoly power on a regional level rather than from firms behaving according to some oligopoly model at the national level.

On the other hand, when dispersion is very low, that is, when an industry's firms are clustered in one or a few areas, nationally-measured concentration has a negative effect on profitability. This finding contradicts the theory that clustering facilitates tacit collusion between firms. There are some possible explanations: first, when firms are located near one another, they serve the same market. In such a case, some model of oligopoly, rather than monopoly, must apply. A finding of zero relationship between concentration and profitability in such a case would imply that firms in oligopolies compete just as fiercely as firms in less concentrated industries. But that would not explain a negative relationship. This could arise because industries that are both concentrated and clustered are highly visible to agents who can extract rents, such as regulators, local tax authorities, or in the case of Russia, mafia groups.

In sum, the Russian data confirm that market structure does affect the competitiveness of industries, but only when market structure is measured to account for the geographical dispersion of industry production in addition to industry concentration. Geographical dispersion seems to allow the firms in concentrated industries to behave like monopolists in regional markets, thus increasing their profitability. On the other hand, clustered oligopolists face lower profits. It is unclear, however, how much of this effect is due to competition between these firms and how much might be due to rent extraction that is facilitated by the visibility of these firms.

What can the state do for industrial firms?

Notwithstanding the crisis, it appears that Russia is either different or laggard compared to other transition economies in that the growth of output and investment has been much slower and the rate of unemployment has been low. Substantial resource reallocation and restructuring are usually considered as a precondition for economic upturn, but they have not been happening. Remedies depend, of course, on the diagnosis: pointing to the slow inter-sectoral reallocation, a revival of sector-specific industrial policies could be advocated; or stressing the slow restructuring, the blame could be attached to the lack of an appropriate environment – competition in goods markets and a strong regulatory framework.

Irena Grosfeld and Claudia Senik-Leygonie's research addresses the issue of the relevant level of intervention and whether targeted industrial policy is desirable in Russia today. Industrial policy seeks to influence either the industrial structure or the general mechanism of production and resource allocation, and so they distinguish two extreme poles of intervention: direct vertical intervention, that is, branch-targeted; and horizontal, across the board, growth-facilitating intervention.

They conclude that the role that the state has to play is more clearly stated in terms of 'modern industrial policy': by implementing horizontal measures that enable firms to undertake restructuring measures. But the problem is that the resumption of growth depends in the last resort on the behaviour of firms and to date, there has been no 'regime change': the adverse behaviour of firms in the old state sector, dominated by insiders, has not improved since the beginning of the transition.

Policies to encourage restructuring

In contrast with most Russian firms, firms in the Central European countries have restructured. Whether state-owned, corporatized or privatized, they reacted to increased product market competition and a hardening of the budget constraint.

Their adjustment was mainly defensive, but the survival-oriented strategy of the state-owned sector led to significant downsizing and asset sales. This facilitated the transfer of assets to more productive uses and contributed to the new private sector development. Moreover, contrary to the initial concern that new private firms would be crowded out by the established state-owned firms, the credit market for the former proved to be quite dynamic and the new private firms do not seem to suffer from credit rationing.

What are the conditions that could trigger this parallel process of downsizing of the old state sector and the expansion of the new private sector in Russia? Several policy measures are necessary to modify people's expectations and increase the credibility of a regime change. Beyond obvious tasks, such as creation of transparent rules of the game, elimination of arbitrariness and corruption, and enforcement of contracts, there are a number of measures focusing more directly on the enterprise sector, which appear to be prerequisites for a radical change in firms' behaviour. It seems that three major factors have been crucial in the Central European countries and these could be useful in Russia, though all of course depend on the existence of a strong and reliable state that can make rules credible and enforceable.

Increased competition in the product market

Import competition has clearly played a role in Russia but competition policy needs to be properly used. Among other things, it must deal with the formation of new types of large and strong organizations, such as FIGs. The development of FIGs has been strongly motivated by the attempt to shelter individual firms from market uncertainties and to avoid liquidity constraints. But they can undermine competition by practising collusive and rent-seeking behaviour. They can easily lobby the government for protection, subsidies and privileged credits. And as they grow, they may become too big to fail. Company failure within such groups is less apparent and can be masked through cross-subsidization.

The creation of large non-state groups should not be forbidden as long as they are subject to anti-monopoly laws and can reasonably claim that the proposed structures will bring about substantial gains in efficiency. But these groups should not be encouraged by special fiscal advantages.

The hardening of bank–firm credit

This must involve not only supervision and regulation of the financial sector, but also the creation of adequate incentives for commercial banks to enforce hard budget constraints on their borrowers and to initiate bankruptcy procedures. For this to happen, commercial bank debt should be a high priority. At present, creditors do not have enough leverage over enterprises and their protection is weak. If banks became harder on bad debtors and settled the debt of established enterprises, the new private sector may find it easier to finance its growth. This would strongly improve the environment for small and medium-size enterprises. Instead of integration with FIGs, smaller firms would then be able to get credit from commercial banks, as happened in the Central European countries.

Enforcement of bankruptcy laws

The credible threat of bankruptcy may change the expectations of employees and managers and encourage them to adopt various measures, including scaling down production and employment to avoid insolvency. Then, in assessing the risks facing their firms, managers can incorporate the possibility of closure.

In the Central European countries, such a change in perception has indirectly contributed not only to significant downsizing but also to a change in ownership structure. For example, in the case of employee buy-outs in Poland, the fear of bankruptcy if the firm failed to restructure has often motivated the search for active outside investors. Bankruptcy should thus become credible enough to impose restructuring. It might help impose financial discipline and preserve those enterprises that are able to undertake organizational and financial restructuring.

Non-enforcement of bankruptcy procedures often comes from the fear of massive, politically unsustainable waves of lay-offs. But even without official bankruptcies, employees can become *de facto* unemployed; for example, by no longer receiving their wages. Moreover, the dynamic impact of liquidations on employment may be positive by transferring assets to more productive uses, thereby contributing to an increased demand for labour. The functioning of the labour market may also be indirectly influenced by the existence of a system of bankruptcy. Employees may accept reductions in employment and foreclosures more easily if they know that their claims for unpaid wages and pension benefits will be satisfied according to a transparent rule.

Lastly, the heterogeneity in managerial competence points to the importance of managerial change and the likely positive impact of new human capital on enterprise performance. Managerial change can be stimulated by the introduction of some elements of contestability; for example, through open bidding for control of a firm. In particular, in the case of insolvency, enterprises should cease to be controlled by incumbent managers.

6 Labour Market Reform

The adjustment of Russia's labour market has been rather different from that of other transition economies. In particular, the growth of the unemployment rate has been much slower, especially given the drastic fall in output. According to the conventional view, this can be explained by a number of factors: the absence of an unemployment benefit scheme; rather generous severance payments compared to unemployment benefits; and the 'demonetization' of the economy, in particular the build-up of wage arrears.

The lesson that economists have tended to derive from these observations is that Russian employers prefer to adapt through prices and not through quantities: instead of laying off redundant workers, employers prefer not to pay wages on a regular basis. It is argued that this behaviour is a rational response to labour market regulations that make it easier to cut wages than to fire people. This behaviour is thought to be matched by the supply side: since unemployment benefits are very low, many workers are unwilling to quit their firms, even if wages are low or not being paid at all.

This chapter focuses on the urgent need for reform of the Russian labour market, especially in the light of the crisis, which revealed the substantial structural problems of the economy and the need to reallocate labour and restructure manufacturing. The chapter briefly summarizes research by Guido Friebel and John Earle presented at the RECEP conference. Earle examines the critical issue of wage arrears (see Earle and Sabirianova, 1998) while Friebel explores the need to restore the rule of law in industrial relations (see Friebel, 1998).

Wage arrears

Although the precise figures are somewhat debatable, there is little doubt that average real wages have declined rather more and employment levels rather less in Russia than in other transition economies. According to Earle and Sabirianova, however, this empirical observation and the conventional inference that Russian labour markets are therefore somehow more 'flexible' fail to explain much of Russian labour market development in the transition period.

Earle and Sabirianova examine the emergence of one of the most puzzling features: wage arrears. The widespread delays in wage payments by Russian employers have taken on particular social and political importance in light of the high and variable inflation rates of the 1990s, when even a short postponement in payment could bring about a large real wage decline as well as considerable uncertainty for workers. Unpaid wages have provoked large strikes and demonstrations; they have been the focus of anti-reform groups emphasizing the social costs of transition to a market economy; and they have been a major point of conflict among Russian political parties and even within the government.

For economists, wage arrears are puzzling for a number of reasons. For a start, the problem is by no means confined to the state budget or certain remote areas, but is widespread in many sectors, regions and types of organizations in Russia. According to aggregate figures from the state statistical committee, the stock of wage arrears totalled R50 trillion on 1 January 1998, with the state budget accounting for only 10% of the total and the rest spread across various industries, notably mining, manufacturing and agriculture.

Research on Russian labour markets has generally treated wage arrears as an indirect way of cutting wages in order to avoid lay-offs. But this does not explain why Russian managers are unusual in choosing wage reductions over quantity (employment and hours) reductions, nor is it clear why managers would choose to pay the same nominal wages late rather than reducing them directly or simply permitting inflation to diminish them in real terms. Paying late is hardly a standard way of cutting labour costs in market economies. What makes Russia different?

Earle and Sabirianova's research suggests that the patterns and persistence of Russian wage arrears reflect a locally stable but inefficient equilibrium, one in which firms pay late and workers tolerate late payment, even though there may exist an alternative, more efficient equilibrium in which workers are paid on time. Their hypothesis starts with the observation that a combination of peculiar conditions have tended to raise the attractiveness of adjustment through wage arrears relative to other forms of adjustment. Even if many firms would prefer not to pay their workers, the sustainability of a wage arrears equilibrium requires that workers accept late payment, at least over some time horizon.

According to Earle and Sabirianova, self-enforcement of wage arrears comes about because the managerial decision to pay wages late has externalities for other firms considering a late payment strategy, particularly those operating in the same local labour market: workers are less likely to quit a firm paying late when other firms in the region also pay late. A generalized wage arrears equilibrium can thus be sustained on a regional level when a critical mass of employers in the region all pay wages late.

The researchers provide evidence for his hypothesis, including the first indications of the existence of intra-firm as well as inter-firm variation in arrears. This suggests that managers are not reluctant to discriminate among different types of workers. The research also shows that arrears tend to be quite concentrated regionally, and indeed that the past regional wage arrears environment and other local labour market conditions greatly raise the expected probability and magnitude of late wage payments.

The research discerns little impact of arrears on the supply of hours: it appears that most unpaid workers continue to work the same hours at the same jobs, although it is not possible to evaluate the impact on their morale and effort. Real effects of arrears show up in some other areas, however. Individuals experiencing arrears on the primary job are more likely to engage in secondary employment activities, to want to change jobs, to sell shares in their company, to experience financial and health problems, and to vote for an anti-reformist presidential candidate.

What is to be done about wage arrears? Earle and Sabirianova certainly do not advocate a bail-out of firms by the state so that the former can meet their contractual obligations. Such a policy might only aggravate future tendencies to non-payment, in anticipation of another bail-out in the future. If there is a role for government action, it would involve first, meeting its own obligations to its employees in order to try to re-establish a standard of punctual payment, and also attempting to enforce contractual obligations on other employers

It seems that moving from the wage arrears equilibrium to a punctual payment equilibrium may be very difficult, given the positive feedback loop that wage arrears seem to create. One negative feedback is the increased tendency that wage arrears create for individuals to enter self-employment, frequently small trading or subsistence agriculture. Wage arrears may finally end when no one is still employed in the large state-owned and formerly state-owned farms and factories.

Labour regulation

Labour relations are mainly regulated by the KZOT, the Russian labour code, created in 1971. Among other things, the code regulates recruitment and separation, the allocation of workers within a firm, and working time. Regulation mainly aims to protect employees from discrimination and provides some *de jure* protection from firing. In order to be able to fire a worker, the employer must prove the worker's unwillingness to work, his or her lack of qualifications, alcohol intoxication or thefts of the firm's property. Moreover, there are many constraints on mass lay-offs and anti-discriminatory rules for women (in particular, for pregnant women), young people and concerning race, religion and ideology.

Although the labour code has been revised several times since 1992, and complemented by federal laws and presidential decrees, labour relations are in substance still regulated by Soviet law. In particular, the code builds on a notion of labour relations that appears to be counterproductive for an economy in transition. Its main goal seems to be to protect employees from discrimination and to make sure that everybody is employed according to their qualifications. The code does not take into account that Russian firms today operate in a completely different framework and that they know that enforcement of rules is weak. Hence, many firms circumvent the regulations. It is, however, remarkable that the labour code is not restrictive concerning wage-setting: wages are not subject to any regulations, except that they must exceed a very low minimum wage.

Collective agreements are the second regulatory basis of the Russian labour market. At the federal level, these are negotiated every year by the Tripartite Commission, consisting of the government, the all-Russian Trade Union, and the all-Russian Employers' Association. Agreements remain very general and consist mainly of non-enforceable directives on labour and social policies. Other collective agreements can be signed for specific sectors, specifying working conditions and minimum wages. There are also agreements at regional and enterprise levels: such agreements must not worsen an employee's position relative to legislation and collective agreements at higher levels.

Enforcement

The labour code stipulates a high degree of employee protection, particularly regarding job security. Paradoxically, these rather protective written laws coincide with insufficient enforcement of employee rights. Although civil courts (there are no specialized labour courts in Russia) decide mostly in favour of employees and workers, there is a lack of enforcement of court decisions, and disorganized trade unions do not fulfil their function as representatives of the workforce. As a consequence, employees tend to be underprotected rather than overprotected.

From 1994–7, the number of lawsuits brought to Russia's civil courts roughly doubled. While in 1994, only 6.8% of the cases brought to civil courts were labour-related, this proportion increased to 34.8% in 1997. The dramatic increase of approximately 900,000 cases in 1996–7 was mostly due to labour cases. While the number of cases that concerned lost jobs were constant, the number of lawsuits filed by employees who were not paid their wages had increased by a factor of 13 since 1994. In 1997, 2% of the labour force of 65 million were involved in lawsuits with their employers.

The wage arrears problem thus has clear repercussions on the legal system. An increasing number of employees are filing lawsuits in order to force their employer to pay their wages. Since the capacity of civil courts has at best been kept constant since 1994, this tendency must necessarily lead to a crowding-out of other cases.

With lost jobs, courts only decide two thirds of the cases in favour of the plaintiff. But in cases of unpaid wages, they have become increasingly employee-friendly, and a decision in favour of the employee has become more or less the default. Courts appear to take into account that wage arrears have become an unlawful but widespread way of enterprises to adjust to shocks. Firing is still a rare event, which may actually be a well-founded decision by firms: in 1997, more than 90% of cases related to unpaid wages were concluded within the deadline stipulated by law, while this was not possible in around 45% of lost job cases. The latter seem to be more complicated and require more attention.

Why then have wage arrears been increasing given that courts are favourable towards employees? First, court capacity is limited. Second, it takes considerable effort for an employee to file a lawsuit. In many parts of Russia, firms are still monopsonists in regional labour markets. Hence, employees and workers may incur high costs when they confront their employer.

Most importantly, however, there are no penalties for firms that lose lawsuits. The maximum a firm can lose in a lawsuit is the wages due and the costs of the litigation. Unless there are penalties, lawsuits can have no deterrent effect on employers. Moreover, there is evidence that even after a lawsuit has been won, employees are not paid the wages due. This is because most firms do not have the cash necessary and are also often highly indebted to suppliers and the tax authorities.

Reforming the regulatory framework of industrial relations

Friebel argues that two principles must be followed when reforming the regulatory framework:

- The new labour code must be appropriate for the current situation. It should focus on protection against accidents, some minimal protection of minors and ill people, and should mainly ensure the payment of wages. The code must not have any regulations that reduce mobility and excessive job protection must be avoided since Russia's labour market must become more mobile.
- The new code must be enforceable, that is, it should be simple. The capacity of courts must be enhanced. In particular, specialized labour courts should be created. Firms can only be forced to follow the law if courts have sanctions, which may even include bankruptcy as a last resort.

Collective bargaining may be an important instrument to make industrial relations more efficient. But when employment and wages are low and/or declining, it cannot be expected that participation will increase. Indeed, the functioning of collective bargaining requires the rule of law as much as individual contracts between firms and workers. The government cannot assume a convincing role in the stimulation of these institutions unless it manages to regain the trust of both employees and entrepreneurs.

7 Russia's Barter Economy

One of the striking features of Russia's economic transition has been the enormous growth in the use of barter. What was a passing phase of transition in Central Europe has become an endemic feature of the Russian situation. The economy has experienced 'redemonetization': in 1992, barter accounted for around 5% of enterprise transactions, but by 1997 this had increased to at least 47%. Estimates of barter turnover vary from 30–80% of inter-enterprise transactions. Barter is also used in paying taxes to local, regional and even federal governments. Even wages are occasionally paid in kind (see Friebel and Guriev, 1999).

The emergence of barter as a stable institution of exchange is a challenge to modern economic theory. Introductory textbooks suggest that barter is inferior to monetary exchange in terms of transaction costs and this is why it is so rare in modern economies. But Russian reality is diametrically opposed to the conventional wisdom. As research by Sergei Guriev and Barry Ickes indicates, Russian enterprises *prefer* to use barter even when they have a choice to pay in cash (see Guriev and Ickes, 1999a,b). Their work, summarized in this chapter, seeks to answer some key questions: why is the Russian economy demonetized? Is this situation good or bad? Is it possible to remonetize it and, if so, how? And is Russia especially vulnerable to barter or can its demonetization disease spread to other countries?

A standard approach to understanding what causes barter is to ask enterprise directors about their motivation. Research using this approach finds that directors see liquidity as the major determinant of barter: enterprise A's director says that his enterprise delivers output to enterprise B in exchange for goods rather than money because enterprise B does not have cash.

But the response of enterprise B's director's may be biased: not that he is necessarily being dishonest, but it is possible that even if he has cash, he might prefer to use it for other purposes, given the knowledge that enterprise A will accept payment in kind. So enterprise B's director has no incentive - and probably has a disincentive – to show his cash, and the lack of cash may be endogenous: the assumption of enterprise A's director that cash is lacking is a large part of the reason why it is lacking. Respondents to surveys may thus overstate the liquidity problems of their counterparts.

To cope with potential bias in directors' responses, Guriev and Ickes take an alternative approach. They start with directors' estimates of how much of their enterprises' revenues take the form of cash and barter and match this data with the enterprise's financial accounts. They then use regression analysis to find out what characteristics of an enterprise make it use barter.

Every enterprise uses barter

The researchers' data on the proportions of revenues in cash and non-cash form are taken from a survey of directors of large industrial enterprises in all industries conducted in the autumn of 1996, 1997 and 1998 by the Centre for Business Trends at the Institute of Economy in Transition. This dataset is then matched with the Goskomstat database of Russian enterprises, which contains the financial accounts of all large and medium-size industrial enterprises. The measure of barter used is the share of barter in sales and there are also data on the share of barter in payments for the enterprises' inputs. These two statistics are very highly correlated.

The share of barter differs across industries but the difference is not statistically significant. One of the stereotypes regarding the Russian economy is that it is clearly split into 'real' and 'virtual' (or 'market' and 'non-market') economies. The idea is that some enterprises use only money while others use only barter. But the data are inconsistent with this picture of a sharply segmented economy, suggesting rather that Russian enterprises use a mixture of monetary and non-monetary means of payment. Some enterprises are always paid in money, but the vast majority of enterprises are paid both in barter and money.

The share of barter in sales is distributed rather uniformly over a broad range. The largest number of enterprises fall in a range of 50–70% of barter. But the data indicate that shares of 10–20% are as common as 70–80%. One implication of this broad variety of barter experience is that the choice of whether or not to use barter is an element of *strategy* for the enterprise. Because the effective price paid depends on the means of payment, enterprises try to pay with goods when they can, reserving use of money for those transactions where cash is essential. The resulting shares of barter across industries reflect market conditions and the opportunities facing enterprises.

Explaining the use of barter

The first hypothesis Guriev and Ickes check is the relationship between barter and the lack of liquidity. Most surveys find that liquidity problems are the leading explanation for barter in Russia but these researchers' evidence calls this conclusion into question. Their results suggest that there is no relationship between the financial position of an enterprise and the likelihood of barter, and there is no significant correlation between barter and availability of liquid assets. The analysis also confirms that barter is not explained by liquidity problems: controlling for all other determinants of barter, neither the share of barter in payments for inputs nor the share of barter in sales are dependent on the stock or flow of liquid assets scaled by annual sales revenue.

It appears that enterprises that have a choice to pay in cash or kind prefer to keep the cash and pay in kind. This is consistent with the hypothesis that the transaction costs structure of the Russian economy is upside down: monetary transactions are more costly than barter. There are numerous explanations for the high costs of monetary transactions in Russia: high taxes, insecure property rights, imperfect credit markets, and rent-seeking by banks and other intermediaries (see Guriev and Pospelov, 1998).

In introductory economics textbooks, money is supposed to be superior to barter because barter exchanges require a double coincidence of wants between the counterparties. But modern information technologies can help lower the search costs significantly. In order to estimate the importance of the double coincidence of wants problem in Russia, Guriev and Ickes use an 'input complexity variable', which measures how many inputs an enterprise needs to produce its output. The more inputs an enterprise needs, the more searches an enterprise would have to undertake when it chooses to sell for barter. Hence, if double coincidence of wants were a problem, enterprises with greater input complexity would be more averse to barter. Controlling for other factors that determine barter, it is clear that enterprises with greater complexity do not have less barter. It seems that the costs associated with arranging complex multilateral barter schemes are overstated, at least in the case of Russia.

There are two factors that help to explain the widespread use of multilateral barter in Russia. First, the widespread emergence of intermediaries that specialize in such barter schemes reduces their cost. Second, many enterprises engage in complex barter arrangements based on relationships inherited from Soviet times. The greater contractual complexity associated with complex barter chains suggests that a history of relationships is important to support these transactions. Because restructuring often involves changes in suppliers and customers, barter may weaken incentives to restructure. It may be a force 'conserving' relationships among enterprises. The emergence of specialized intermediaries and the survival of Soviet industrial links could add up to a 'lock-in' effect, which helps perpetuate barter. The empirical evidence is consistent with this hypothesis.

The researchers find that there are considerable economies of scale in barter transactions: a 10% increase in an enterprise's size (measured by sales revenue) results in a 0.25% increase in the share of barter in sales. Combined with the complexity result, this provides an insight into the nature of barter transaction costs in Russia. The barter market is so comprehensive that everything can be bought for payments in kind and therefore virtually every product can be used as a means of payment. But in order to join the barter network, an enterprise has to pay a fixed entry cost, most commonly to hire a 'barter broker'. It could also be that larger enterprises are more likely to be older, and involved in inherited barter chains. New, smaller enterprises cannot afford to join the barter network or cannot find a vacant niche in it. Hence the size–barter relationship.

The other empirical finding is that besides static economies of scale, there are *dynamic* economies of scale in barter: an enterprise that uses more barter today is more likely to use barter tomorrow. This could be due to learning by doing, or simply to fixed costs associated with forming barter relationships: once formed, the marginal cost of maintaining barter is much lower.

Barter has become so common that even exporters and foreign-owned enterprises have become involved in it. It is irrelevant whether an enterprise is public or private, and whether it has domestic or foreign owners. The analysis confirms that ownership does not matter: all ownership types use barter to roughly the same extent. Access to global markets has a small impact on barter. It would be expected that an enterprise exporting one more rouble of its output abroad would sell one less rouble for barter. But then the enterprise would have to pay cash for its own inputs, which is more costly. The data support this hypothesis: an increase of one rouble in exports leads to a decrease of as little as 17 kopecks in barter sales. It might be that these are the 'wrong' exports, that is, exports to cash-constrained CIS countries, but the distinction between CIS and non-CIS exports turns out to be insignificant.

Barter is higher in enterprises whose directors resist restructuring. Enterprises that shed labour and increase labour productivity have a lower share of barter, while those that keep excess labour even when their output is falling have a greater share of barter. The empirical analysis is therefore consistent with the idea that Russian directors have a choice either to invest in restructuring or to invest in relationship capital. The former increases productivity while the latter facilitates barter exchanges.

Copious anecdotal evidence suggests that the greatest amount of barter is concentrated in natural monopolies. Guriev and Kvasov (1999) build a model, which shows that willingness to accept barter payment helps monopolies to discriminate between their customers. The model predicts that greater market power leads to more barter. It also suggests that in the case of oligopoly, there are multiple equilibria: one with barter and one without barter. The barter equilibrium can only exist if markets are sufficiently concentrated. The empirical evidence is consistent with this model: barter is lower in more competitive industries. Moreover, if the concentration ratio is below a certain threshold, the share of barter falls abruptly to very low levels.

Is barter good or bad?

Economists and policy-makers have been insisting that the barter economy is an evil. But the fact that many enterprises prefer to use barter instead of money implies that locally, in individual buyer–seller transactions, barter is more efficient than money. By checking whether enterprises perform better or worse in the next year if they use more barter in the current year, Guriev and Ickes find that current involvement in barter does not worsen the future prospects of an enterprise.

But the proliferation of barter imposes a huge externality on the economy as a whole. By definition, barter transactions are much less observable and are therefore less taxable. Governments of all levels respond by collecting taxes in kind, but the impossibility of measuring the value of these payments creates a source of bureaucratic discretion that leads to corruption. Therefore, barter hits government revenues hard and strips the economy of public spending.

Barter may also act as an entry barrier. If barter is more common among enterprises that have been long-term trading partners, then it makes it hard for enterprises to enter into new relationships. Hence, widespread use of barter may hinder restructuring and competition.

Policy implications

The key results of Guriev and Ickes' empirical analysis are that the likelihood that an enterprise will engage in barter is independent of its financial position; and that barter is more common in larger enterprises and in more concentrated industries. These findings imply that since the search costs of finding countertrade partners are very low, the Russian economy may be in a barter trap where barter is so common that it is less costly to carry out exchanges without money.

One policy implication that can be drawn from this is that merely printing money will not help to decrease barter. If the government wants to reduce barter, it should undertake serious institutional changes. Otherwise, an increase in nominal money supply will result in inflation, and real money supply will be the same with inter-enterprise transactions remaining at the same level of demonetization.

The results raise a legitimate question: why is barter prevalent in Russia, while it is virtually non-existent in other economies (though see Kaufmann and Marin, 1998, for discussion of barter deals in Ukraine)? Rent-seeking is high in Russia, but there are other countries with insecure property rights. Russian markets are concentrated, but not much more concentrated than in many other countries (see Brown and Brown, 1998).

One possible explanation for the peculiarity of the Russian experience is the existence of multiple equilibria. For the same setting, there may be at least two stable equilibria: one with barter and one without. There may be a path-dependence effect, where history determines the outcome. In 1995, a liquidity shock threw the economy into the barter trap, a high barter equilibrium. Since that time, price flexibility should have restored an equilibrium level of real money stock but the real money supply is now three times lower than it used to be. So the Russian economy is in the institutional trap of barter.

The multiple equilibria argument is quite common in the modern literature on transition and development. It is basically the cornerstone of the so-called 'post-Washington consensus' that is gradually replacing the Washington consensus on economic transition. The post-Washington consensus states that institutions, which matter a great deal for transition, may fail to emerge spontaneously. Government then needs to intervene to promote good institutions or the economy will find itself in a low-level equilibrium.

But what Guriev and Ickes' analysis suggests is not simply a restatement of the idea that Russia may be in a low-level equilibrium. They find that at some level of competitiveness, the barter equilibrium disappears and industry jumps to the no-barter equilibrium. This argument suggests non-trivial policy implications. In order to reduce barter, the government should promote competition. Moreover, even if competition policy may have had little effect on barter so far, the government should not give up. Barter may fall dramatically when a certain threshold level of competition is achieved.

Bibliography

Ahrend, R. (1999), 'Russia's Post-Stabilization Decline, Crash and Revival', *Russian Economic Trends* 8 (3).

Brown, A. and Brown, D. (1998), 'The Evolution of Industrial Structure in Russia: Implications for Competition', paper presented at the RECEP conference, Moscow, 11–12 September.

Brown, D., Guriev, S. and Volchkova, N. (1999), 'Financial–Industrial Groups in Russia: Virtue or Vice', *Russian Economic Trends* 8 (3).

Earle, J. (1998), 'Russia Defaulted Long Ago', paper presented at the RECEP conference, Moscow, 11–12 September.

Earle, J. and Sabirianova, K. (1998), 'Understanding Wage Arrears in Russia', paper presented at the RECEP conference, Moscow, 11–12 September.

Friebel, G. (1998), 'The Russian Labour Market: Urgent Needs for Reform', paper presented at the RECEP conference, Moscow, 11–12 September.

Friebel, G. and Guriev, S. (1999), 'Why Russian Workers Do Not Move: Attachment of Workers Through Payment in Kind', mimeo, RECEP.

Fries, S., Neven, D., Ng, C. and Seabright, P. (1998), 'The Performance of the Banking System in Transition', paper presented at the RECEP conference, Moscow, 11–12 September.

Gorban, M. and Westin, P. (1999), 'Next Year's Budget: The First Reading', *Russian Economic Trends*, Monthly Update, October.

Grosfeld, I. and Senik-Leygonie, C. (1998), 'Industrial Policy in the Russian Transition: What can the State do for Industrial Firms?', paper presented at the RECEP conference, Moscow, 11–12 September.

Guriev, S. and Ickes, B. (1999a), 'Barter in Russian Enterprises: Myths versus Empirical Evidence', *Russian Economic Trends*. 8 (2).

Guriev, S. and Ickes, B. (1999b), 'Non-Monetary Transactions in Russian Economy', Final Report of GET Research Project, New Economic School.

Guriev, S. and Kvasov, D. (1999), 'Barter in Russia: The Role of Market Power', mimeo, New Economic School.

Guriev, S. and Pospelov, I. (1998), 'A Model of Russia's Virtual Economy: Transactions Costs, Quasi-Money, Barter and Mutual Credit', paper presented at the RECEP conference, Moscow, 11–12 September.

Ivanova, N. and Wyplosz, C. (1998), 'Arrears: The Tide that is Drowning Russia', paper presented at the RECEP conference, Moscow, 11–12 September; updated summary in *Russian Economic Trends* 8 (1).

Johnson, S., McMillan, J. and Woodruff, C. (1998), 'Job Creation in the Private Sector: Poland, Russia, Slovakia and Ukraine Compared', paper presented at the RECEP conference, Moscow, 11–12 September.

Kaufmann, D. and Marin, D. (1998), 'Disorganization, Financial Squeeze and Barter', paper presented at the RECEP conference, Moscow, 11–12 September.

Lavrov, A. (1996), 'Fiscal Federalism and Financial Stabilization', *Problems of Economic Transition*.

MacFarquhar, R. (1998), 'Can't Tax or Won't Tax?: Russia's Tax Effort and the August 17 Financial Crisis', paper presented at the RECEP conference, Moscow, 11–12 September.

Neven, D. (1998), 'The Impact of Import Penetration on Market Structure and Enterprise Performance', paper presented at the RECEP conference, Moscow, 11–12 September.

Neven, D., Bessonova, Z. and Gorban, M. (1998), 'Enterprise Restructuring in the Russian Manufacturing Sector 1992–6: An Overview', paper presented at the RECEP conference, Moscow, 11–12 September.

Perotti, E. (1999a), 'Financial–Industrial Groups and Financial Crisis: Lessons for Russia', *The Stockholm Report on Transition* 10 (1).

Perotti, E. (1999b), 'A Strategy for Jump-Starting Bank Restructuring in Russia', mimeo, University of Amsterdam.

Perotti, E. and Gelfer, S. (1998), 'Investment Financing in Russian Financial-Industrial Groups', paper presented at the RECEP conference, Moscow, 11–12 September.

RECEP (1998), 'What Went Wrong', *Russian Economic Trends*, Monthly Update, September.

Treisman, D. (1996), 'The Politics of Intergovernmental Transfers in Post-Soviet Russia', *British Journal of Political Science*.

Westin, P. (1999), 'One Year After the Crisis: What Went Right?', *Russian Economic Trends*, Monthly Update, September.

Yudaeva, K. (1998), 'Financial Crises in Emerging Markets', paper presented at the RECEP conference, Moscow, 11–12 September.

Yudaeva, K. and Wyplosz, C. (1998), 'The Cost of Debt Conversion: Russia and Mexico Compared', paper presented at the RECEP conference, Moscow, 11–12 September; and in *Russian Economic Trends* 7 (4).

Zhuravskaya, K. (1998), 'Incentives to Provide Local Public Goods: Fiscal Federalism, Russian Style', paper presented at the RECEP conference, Moscow, 11–12 September.

Zhuravskaya, K. (1999), 'Intergovernmental Relations in Russia', *Russian Economic Trends* 8 (1).